초등학생의 영어 친구

리스닝
버디

LISTENING
BUDDY

3

리스닝버디 3

지은이	NE능률 영어교육연구소
연구원	한정은, 백수자, 권혜진, 송진아, 황선영
영문 교열	Peter Morton, MyAn Le, Lewis Hugh Hosie
디자인	방호현, 장현정, 김연주
내지 일러스트	이은교, 전진희, 김현수
내지 사진	www.shutterstock.com
맥편집	ELIM
영업	한기영, 이경구, 박인규, 정철교, 김남준, 김남형, 이우현
마케팅	박혜선, 고유진, 김여진

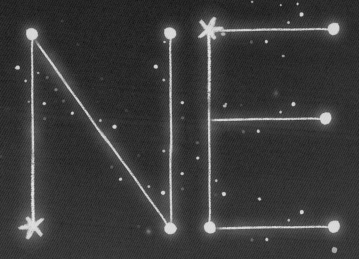

NE능률이 미래를 그립니다.

교육에 대한 큰 꿈을 품고 시작한 NE능률
처음 품었던 그 꿈을 잊지 않고 40년이 넘는 시간 동안 한 길만을 걸어왔습니다.

이제 NE능률이 앞으로 나아가야 할 길을 그려봅니다.
'평범한 열 개의 제품보다 하나의 탁월한 제품'이라는
변치 않는 철학을 바탕으로 진정한 배움의 가치를 알리는
NE능률이 교육의 미래를 열어가겠습니다.

NE 능률 www.neungyule.com

초등학생의 영어 친구

리스닝 버디 단어장

3

NE능률

초등학생의 영어 친구

리스닝 버디 단어장

3

NE 능률

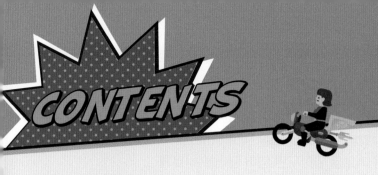

CONTENTS

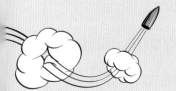

발음 기호를 배워 봅시다.

하나의 알파벳이 여러 소리를 가지고 있는 경우가 있어서, 같은 알파벳이라도
단어에 따라 소리가 달라져요. 하지만 발음 기호를 알아두면 영어 단어를 바르게
읽을 수 있답니다. 듣고 따라 하면서 발음 기호를 익혀봅시다.

★ 자음 ★

기호	단어
p	pizza [píːtsə]
b	brother [brʌ́ðər]
t	tall [tɔːl]
d	day [dei]
k	key [kiː]
g	glad [glæd]
tʃ	choose [tʃuːz]
dʒ	jacket [dʒǽkit]
s	see [siː]
z	zoo [zuː]
ʃ	shoes [ʃuːz]
ʒ	pleasure [pléʒər]
h	have [hæv]
m	morning [mɔ́ːrniŋ]
n	name [neim]
ŋ	sing [siŋ]
f	family [fǽməli]
v	violin [vàiəlín]

기호	단어
θ	throw [θrou]
ð	this [ðis]
l	lizard [lízərd]
r	rabbit [rǽbit]
j	yes [jes]
w	want [wɑnt]

★ 모음 ★

기호	단어
a	doctor [dáktər]
e	pet [pet]
i	meet [miːt]
o	go [gou]
u	blue [bluː]
æ	cat [kæt]
ʌ	fun [fʌn]
ɔ	long [lɔ(ː)ŋ]
ə	crayon [kréiən]
ɛ	wear [wɛər]

UNIT 1 PEOPLE AROUND ME

WORDS

듣고 따라 말해 봅시다.

☐ **tall** [tɔːl]	키가 큰	☐ **funny** [fʌ́ni]	재미있는
☐ **short** [ʃɔːrt]	키가 작은	☐ **lazy** [léizi]	게으른
☐ **thin** [θin]	날씬한	☐ **hair** [hɛər]	머리카락
☐ **fat** [fæt]	뚱뚱한	☐ **friendly** [fréndli]	친절한
☐ **shy** [ʃai]	수줍음을 많이 타는	☐ **handsome** [hǽnsəm]	잘생긴
☐ **outgoing** [áutgouiŋ]	외향적인	☐ **kind** [kaind]	친절한

EXPRESSIONS

듣고 따라 말해 봅시다.

☐ A: What does she look like? (그녀는 어떻게 생겼니?)

   B: She is tall and thin. (그녀는 키가 크고 날씬해.)

☐ A: What is she like? (그녀는 어떤 사람이니?)

   B: She is shy. (그녀는 수줍음이 많아.)

WORDS & EXPRESSIONS TEST

A 다음 영어는 한글로, 한글은 영어로 쓰시오.

1 friendly _____

2 funny _____

3 shy _____

4 handsome _____

5 thin _____

6 머리카락 _____

7 게으른 _____

8 외향적인 _____

9 뚱뚱한 _____

10 키가 작은 _____

B 다음 우리말을 바르게 영작하시오.

1 그녀는 어떤 사람이니?

→ _____ _____ _____ _____?

2 그녀는 수줍음이 많아.

→ _____ _____ _____.

3 그녀는 어떻게 생겼니?

→ _____ _____ _____ _____?

4 그녀는 키가 크고 날씬해.

→ _____ _____ _____.

UNIT 2 JOBS

WORDS

듣고 따라 말해 봅시다.

□ **scientist** [sáiəntist]	과학자	□ **chef** [ʃef]	요리사
□ **singer** [síŋər]	가수	□ **vet** [vet]	수의사
□ **police officer**	경찰관	□ **doctor** [dáktər]	의사
□ **firefighter** [fáiərfaitər]	소방관	□ **teacher** [tíːtʃər]	선생님
□ **dentist** [déntist]	치과의사	□ **like** [laik]	좋아하다; ~처럼
□ **pilot** [páilət]	조종사	□ **be proud of**	~을 자랑스러워 하다

EXPRESSIONS

듣고 따라 말해 봅시다.

□ A: What does your father do? (너희 아빠는 무슨 일을 하시니?)

  B: He is a police officer. (경찰관이셔.)

□ A: What do you want to be? (너는 뭐가 되고 싶니?)

  B: I want to be a chef. (나는 요리사가 되고 싶어.)

WORDS & EXPRESSIONS TEST

A 다음 영어는 한글로, 한글은 영어로 쓰시오.

1 singer _____

2 chef _____

3 doctor _____

4 like _____

5 firefighter _____

6 선생님 _____

7 조종사 _____

8 치과의사 _____

9 과학자 _____

10 경찰관 _____

B 다음을 바르게 배열하여 문장을 완성하시오.

1 to be / a chef / want / I / .

→ _____

2 does / do / your / what / father / ?

→ _____

3 a police officer / is / he / .

→ _____

4 you / do / to be / want / what / ?

→ _____

WoW!

UNIT 3 FOUR SEASONS

WORDS

듣고 따라 말해 봅시다.

□ **spring** [spriŋ]	봄	□ **see colorful leaves**	형형색색의 나뭇잎을 보다
□ **summer** [sʌ́mər]	여름	□ **go skiing**	스키 타러 가다
□ **fall** [fɔ:l]	가을	□ **cold** [kould]	추운; 감기
□ **winter** [wíntər]	겨울	□ **hot** [hɑ:t]	더운, 뜨거운
□ **go on a picnic**	소풍을 가다	□ **warm** [wɔ:rm]	따뜻한
□ **play at the beach**	해변에서 놀다	□ **cool** [ku:l]	시원한

EXPRESSIONS

듣고 따라 말해 봅시다.

□ A: Which seasons do you like? (너는 어느 계절을 좋아하니?)

　 B: I like fall. (나는 가을을 좋아해.)

□ A: Why do you like summer? (너는 왜 여름을 좋아하니?)

　 B: Because I can play at the beach. (왜냐하면 해변에서 놀 수 있기 때문이야.)

WORDS & EXPRESSIONS TEST

A 다음 영어는 한글로, 한글은 영어로 쓰시오.

1 fall _____

2 warm _____

3 hot _____

4 spring _____

5 go on a picnic _____

6 겨울 _____

7 추운; 감기 _____

8 스키 타러 가다 _____

9 여름 _____

10 시원한 _____

B 다음 문장을 해석하시오.

1 I like fall.

→ _____

2 Why do you like summer?

→ _____

3 Because I can play at the beach.

→ _____

4 Which seasons do you like?

→ _____

WoW!

UNIT 4 SICKNESS

WORDS

듣고 따라 말해 봅시다.

☐ **headache** [hédèik]	두통	☐ **sore throat**	인후염(목 아픔)
☐ **toothache** [túːθèik]	치통	☐ **see a doctor**	병원에 가다
☐ **stomachache** [stʌ́məkèik]	복통	☐ **take medicine**	약을 먹다
☐ **fever** [fíːvər]	열	☐ **rest** [rest]	쉬다
☐ **cough** [kɔ(ː)f]	기침	☐ **have a cold**	감기에 걸리다
☐ **runny nose**	콧물	☐ **go to school**	학교에 가다

EXPRESSIONS

듣고 따라 말해 봅시다.

☐ A: Are you okay? What's wrong? (너 괜찮니? 어디 아프니?)

B: I have a stomachache. (나 배가 아파.)

☐ A: I have a fever. (나 열이 나.)

B: You should see a doctor. (너 병원에 가야겠다.)

WORDS & EXPRESSIONS TEST

DATE　PARENTS　TEACHER

A 다음 영어는 한글로, 한글은 영어로 쓰시오.

1 cough _____

2 take medicine _____

3 fever _____

4 go to school _____

5 rest _____

6 sore throat _____

7 병원에 가다 _____

8 감기에 걸리다 _____

9 복통 _____

10 콧물 _____

11 치통 _____

12 두통 _____

B 다음 우리말을 바르게 영작하시오.

1 나 열이 나.

→ _____ _____ _____ _____.

2 너 병원에 가야겠다.

→ _____ _____ _____ _____ _____.

3 나 배가 아파.

→ _____ _____ _____ _____.

UNIT 5 AT THE RESTAURANT

WORDS

듣고 따라 말해 봅시다.

□ order [ɔ́ːrdər]	주문하다	□ hamburger [hǽmbə̀ːrgər]	햄버거
□ menu [ménjuː]	메뉴, 식단표	□ French fries	감자튀김
□ bill [bil]	계산서	□ pie [pai]	파이
□ dessert [dizə́ːrt]	디저트, 후식	□ wait a moment	잠깐 기다리다
□ steak [steik]	스테이크	□ delicious [dilíʃəs]	맛있는

EXPRESSIONS

듣고 따라 말해 봅시다.

□ A: Are you ready to order? (주문하시겠어요?)
  B: Yes. I'll have the steak. (네. 스테이크로 할게요.)

□ A: What would you like to have? (너 뭐 먹을래?)
  B: I want the apple pie. (난 사과 파이 먹을래.)

□ A: May I have the bill, please? (계산서 좀 갖다 주시겠어요?)
  B: Sure. Please wait a moment. (물론이죠. 잠시만 기다려 주세요.)

WORDS & EXPRESSIONS TEST

DATE   PARENTS   TEACHER

A 다음 영어는 한글로, 한글은 영어로 쓰시오.

1 bill _____   6 메뉴, 식단표 _____

2 French fries _____   7 파이 _____

3 delicious _____   8 주문하다 _____

4 hamburger _____   9 스테이크 _____

5 wait a moment _____ 10 디저트, 후식 _____

B 다음을 바르게 배열하여 문장을 완성하시오.

1 want / the apple / I / pie / .

→ _____

2 I / the bill / please / may / have / , / ?

→ _____

3 to / ready / you / order / are / ?

→ _____

4 have / I'll / the steak / .

→ _____

UNIT 6 SPECIAL DAYS

WORDS

들고 따라 말해 봅시다.

☐ **January** [dʒǽnjueri]	1월	☐ **July** [dʒulái]	7월
☐ **February** [fébrueri]	2월	☐ **August** [ɔ́:gəst]	8월
☐ **March** [mɑːrtʃ]	3월	☐ **September** [septémbər]	9월
☐ **April** [éiprəl]	4월	☐ **October** [ɑktóubər]	10월
☐ **May** [mei]	5월	☐ **November** [nouvémbər]	11월
☐ **June** [dʒuːn]	6월	☐ **December** [disémbər]	12월

EXPRESSIONS

들고 따라 말해 봅시다.

☐ A: What's the date today? (오늘 며칠이니?)

B: It's November 11 (eleventh). (11월 11일이야.)

☐ A: When is your birthday? (네 생일은 언제니?)

B: It's June 3 (third). (6월 3일이야.)

WORDS & EXPRESSIONS TEST

A 다음 영어는 한글로, 한글은 영어로 쓰시오.

1 March _____　　　　**7** 2월 _____

2 September _____　　**8** 5월 _____

3 April _____　　　　**9** 7월 _____

4 January _____　　　**10** 8월 _____

5 December _____　　**11** 10월 _____

6 June _____　　　　**12** 11월 _____

B 다음 우리말을 바르게 영작하시오.

1 오늘 며칠이니?

→ _____ _____ _____ _____?

2 네 생일은 언제니?

→ _____ _____ _____ _____?

3 6월 3일이야.

→ _____ _____ _____.

UNIT 7 THE PAST

WORDS

듣고 따라 말해 봅시다.

☐ played baseball	야구를 했다	☐ took photos	사진을 찍었다
☐ watched TV	TV를 보았다	☐ had lunch	점심을 먹었다
☐ visited a museum	박물관을 방문했다	☐ last [læst]	지난
☐ went swimming	수영하러 갔다	☐ yesterday [jéstərdei]	어제
☐ had a party	파티를 열었다	☐ weekend [wíːkènd]	주말
☐ took a trip	여행을 갔다	☐ vacation [veikéiʃən]	방학

EXPRESSIONS

듣고 따라 말해 봅시다.

☐ A: What did you do yesterday? (너 어제 뭐 했니?)
  B: I visited a museum. (박물관을 방문했어.)

☐ A: How was your weekend? (주말 어땠니?)
  B: It was a lot of fun. I took a trip with my family.
    (정말 재미있었어. 나는 가족과 여행을 갔었어.)

WORDS & EXPRESSIONS TEST

A 다음 영어는 한글로, 한글은 영어로 쓰시오.

1 had lunch _____

2 yesterday _____

3 took photos _____

4 weekend _____

5 had a party _____

6 방학 _____

7 지난 _____

8 수영하러 갔다 _____

9 야구를 했다 _____

10 TV를 보았다 _____

B 다음을 바르게 배열하여 문장을 완성하시오.

1 museum / I / a / visited / .

→ _____

2 do / what / yesterday / you / did / ?

→ _____

3 was / your / how / weekend / ?

→ _____

4 with / a trip / took / I / family / my / .

→ _____

18

UNIT 8 PHONE CALLS

WORDS

들고 따라 말해 봅시다.

☐ **answer the phone**	전화를 받다	☐ **have the wrong number**	전화를 잘못 걸다
☐ **hold on**	전화를 끊지 않고 기다리다	☐ **tell** [tel]	말하다, 전하다
☐ **leave a message**	메모를 남기다	☐ **meet** [miːt]	만나다
☐ **call back**	다시 전화를 하다	☐ **park** [pɑːrk]	공원
☐ **hang up**	전화를 끊다	☐ **tomorrow** [təmɔ́ːrou]	내일

EXPRESSIONS

들고 따라 말해 봅시다.

☐ A: May I speak to Amy? (Amy와 통화할 수 있을까요?)
 B: Speaking. / She's not at home. (전데요. / 그녀는 집에 없어요.)

☐ A: Who's calling, please? (누구세요?)
 B: This is Mike. (저 Mike예요.)

☐ A: May I leave a message? (메모 남겨도 될까요?)
 B: Sure. (물론이지.)

WORDS & EXPRESSIONS TEST

A 다음 영어는 한글로, 한글은 영어로 쓰시오.

1 hold on   _____

2 call back   _____

3 answer the phone   _____

4 park   _____

5 tomorrow   _____

6 만나다   _____

7 말하다, 전하다   _____

8 전화를 끊다   _____

9 메모를 남기다   _____

10 전화를 잘못 걸다   _____

B 다음 우리말을 바르게 영작하시오.

1 Amy와 통화할 수 있을까요?

   → _____ _____ _____ _____ _____?

2 누구세요?

   → _____ _____, _____?

3 저 Mike예요.

   → _____ _____ _____.

4 메모 남겨도 될까요?

   → _____ _____ _____ _____ _____?

UNIT 9 MY TOWN

WORDS

듣고 따라 말해 봅시다.

□ **library** [láibrəri]	도서관	□ **turn right**	오른쪽으로 돌다
□ **bank** [bæŋk]	은행	□ **go straight**	똑바로 가다
□ **hospital** [háspitəl]	병원	□ **next to**	~ 옆에
□ **bakery** [béikəri]	빵집	□ **between** [bitwí:n]	~의 사이에
□ **movie theater**	영화관	□ **around** [əráund]	주변에
□ **turn left**	왼쪽으로 돌다	□ **understand** [ʌ̀ndərstǽnd]	이해하다

EXPRESSIONS

듣고 따라 말해 봅시다.

□ A: Where is the bakery? (빵집이 어디에 있나요?)

B: It's next to the bank. (은행 옆에 있어요.)

□ A: How can I get to the movie theater? (영화관에 어떻게 가면 되나요?)

B: Go straight and turn left. It will be on your left.
   (똑바로 가서 왼쪽으로 도세요. 왼편에 있을 거예요.)

WORDS & EXPRESSIONS TEST

A 다음 영어는 한글로, 한글은 영어로 쓰시오.

1	bakery	7	도서관
2	around	8	은행
3	hospital	9	~의 사이에
4	movie theater	10	~ 옆에
5	turn left	11	오른쪽으로 돌다
6	understand	12	똑바로 가다

B 다음을 바르게 배열하여 문장을 완성하시오.

1 I / can / movie theater / get to / how / the / ?

→ _____

2 next / bank / to / the / it's / .

→ _____

3 is / the / where / bakery / ?

→ _____

UNIT 10 PLANS

WORDS

듣고 따라 말해 봅시다.

☐ **go shopping**	쇼핑하러 가다	☐ **travel overseas**	해외여행을 하다
☐ **get a haircut**	머리를 자르다	☐ **plan** [plæn]	계획
☐ **relax at home**	집에서 쉬다	☐ **next** [nekst]	다음의
☐ **go camping**	캠핑 가다	☐ **mountain** [máuntən]	산
☐ **study Chinese**	중국어를 공부하다	☐ **exciting** [iksáitiŋ]	신나는

EXPRESSIONS

듣고 따라 말해 봅시다.

☐ A: What are you going to do tomorrow? (너 내일 뭐 할 거니?)
   B: I'm going to get a haircut. (난 머리를 자를 거야.)

☐ A: Do you have any plans for your vacation? (너 방학에 계획 있니?)
   B: Yes, I'm going to go camping with my dad.
      (응, 난 아빠랑 캠핑 갈 거야.)

WORDS & EXPRESSIONS TEST

DATE   PARENTS   TEACHER

A 다음 영어는 한글로, 한글은 영어로 쓰시오.

1 go camping _____

2 get a haircut _____

3 plan _____

4 exciting _____

5 mountain _____

6 다음의 _____

7 해외여행을 하다 _____

8 중국어를 공부하다 _____

9 집에서 쉬다 _____

10 쇼핑하러 가다 _____

B 다음 문장을 해석하시오.

1 What are you going to do tomorrow?

→ _____

2 Do you have any plans for your vacation?

→ _____

3 I'm going to get a haircut.

→ _____

4 I'm going to go camping with my dad.

→ _____

WoW!

부록

☆ NUMBERS

1	one	17	seventeen
2	two	18	eighteen
3	three	19	nineteen
4	four	20	twenty
5	five	21	twenty-one
6	six	22	twenty-two
7	seven	23	twenty-three
8	eight	24	twenty-four
9	nine	30	thirty
10	ten	40	forty
11	eleven	50	fifty
12	twelve	60	sixty
13	thirteen	70	seventy
14	fourteen	80	eighty
15	fifteen	90	ninety
16	sixteen	100	one hundred

 ★ DATES

January

Sunday	Monday	Tuesday	Wednesday	Thursday	Friday	Saturday
1 first	2 second	3 third	4 fourth	5 fifth	6 sixth	7 seventh
8 eighth	9 ninth	10 tenth	11 eleventh	12 twelfth	13 thir-teenth	14 four-teenth
15 fif-teenth	16 six-teenth	17 seven-teenth	18 eigh-teenth	19 nine-teenth	20 twentie-th	21 twenty-first
22 twenty-second	23 twenty-third	24 twenty-fourth	25 twenty-fifth	26 twenty-sixth	27 twenty-seventh	28 twenty-eighth
29 twenty-ninth	30 thirtieth	31 thirty-first			WoW!	

WORDS & EXPRESSIONS TEST 정답

UNIT 1 PEOPLE AROUND ME

P. 6

A 1 친절한 2 재미있는 3 수줍음을 많이 타는
4 잘생긴 5 날씬한 6 hair 7 lazy
8 outgoing 9 fat 10 short

B 1 What, is, she, like
2 She, is, shy
3 What, does, she, look, like
4 She, is, tall, and, thin

UNIT 2 JOBS

P. 8

A 1 가수 2 요리사 3 의사 4 좋아하다; ~처럼
5 소방관 6 teacher 7 pilot 8 dentist
9 scientist 10 police officer

B 1 I want to be a chef.
2 What does your father do?
3 He is a police officer.
4 What do you want to be?

UNIT 3 FOUR SEASONS

P. 10

A 1 가을 2 따뜻한 3 더운, 뜨거운 4 봄
5 소풍을 가다 6 winter 7 cold
8 go skiing 9 summer 10 cool

B 1 나는 가을을 좋아해.
2 너는 왜 여름을 좋아하니?

3 왜냐하면 해변에서 놀 수 있기 때문이야.
4 너는 어느 계절을 좋아하니?

UNIT 4 SICKNESS

P. 12

A 1 기침 2 약을 먹다 3 열 4 학교에 가다
5 쉬다 6 인후염(목 아픔) 7 see a doctor
8 have a cold 9 stomachache
10 runny nose 11 toothache
12 headache

B 1 I, have, a, fever
2 You, should, see, a, doctor
3 I, have, a, stomachache

UNIT 5 AT THE RESTAURANT

P. 14

A 1 계산서 2 감자튀김 3 맛있는 4 햄버거
5 잠깐 기다리다 6 menu 7 pie 8 order
9 steak 10 dessert

B 1 I want the apple pie.
2 May I have the bill, please?
3 Are you ready to order?
4 I'll have the steak.

UNIT 6 SPECIAL DAYS

P. 16

A 1 3월 2 9월 3 4월 4 1월 5 12월

6 6월   7 February   8 May   9 July
10 August   11 October   12 November

B 1 What's, the, date, today
  2 When, is, your, birthday
  3 It's, June, 3 (third)

8 bank   9 between   10 next to
11 turn right   12 go straight

B 1 How can I get to the movie theater?
  2 It's next to the bank.
  3 Where is the bakery?

UNIT 7 THE PAST

P. 18

A 1 점심을 먹었다   2 어제   3 사진을 찍었다
  4 주말   5 파티를 열었다   6 vacation   7 last
  8 went swimming   9 played baseball
  10 watched TV

B 1 I visited a museum.
  2 What did you do yesterday?
  3 How was your weekend?
  4 I took a trip with my family.

UNIT 10 PLANS

P. 24

A 1 캠핑 가다   2 머리를 자르다   3 계획   4 신나는
  5 산   6 next   7 travel overseas
  8 study Chinese   9 relax at home
  10 go shopping

B 1 너 내일 뭐 할 거니?
  2 너 방학에 계획 있니?
  3 난 머리를 자를 거야.
  4 난 아빠랑 캠핑 갈 거야.

UNIT 8 PHONE CALLS

P. 20

A 1 전화를 끊지 않고 기다리다   2 다시 전화를 하다
  3 전화를 받다   4 공원   5 내일   6 meet
  7 tell   8 hang up   9 leave a message
  10 have the wrong number

B 1 May, I, speak, to, Amy
  2 Who's, calling, please
  3 This, is, Mike
  4 May, I, leave, a, message

UNIT 9 MY TOWN

P. 22

A 1 빵집   2 주변에   3 병원   4 영화관
  5 왼쪽으로 돌다   6 이해하다   7 library

초등학생의 영어 친구
리스닝버디
LISTENING BUDDY 3

Dear Friends,

I'm your English Buddy!
Forget about all your worries.
I'm here to help you!
Let's smile! Let's learn! And let's have fun!

All the best,
Your English Buddy

★ HOW TO USE ★

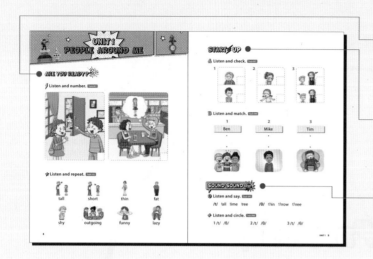

ARE YOU READY

그림을 보면서 본문에서 다룰 주요 단어와 표현을 학습합니다.

START UP

간단한 문제를 통해 학습한 단어와 표현을 확인합니다.

SOUND SOUND

주의해야 할 발음과 억양을 듣고 따라 함으로써 올바른 영어 발음을 익힐 수 있습니다.

LISTEN UP

반복적·단계적으로 구성된 대화를 듣고 연습 문제를 풀어봄으로써, 주요 의사소통 기능을 자연스럽게 습득할 수 있습니다.

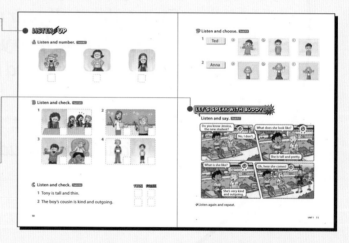

LET'S SPEAK WITH BUDDY

재미있는 만화와 함께 배운 표현들을 복습합니다. 제시된 대체 어휘들을 이용하여 친구와 역할극을 해 봅니다.

DICTATION

앞에서 학습한 내용을 다시 한 번 듣고 받아 써 봅니다. 단어, 문장, 대화 순으로 체계적인 받아 쓰기 학습을 할 수 있습니다.

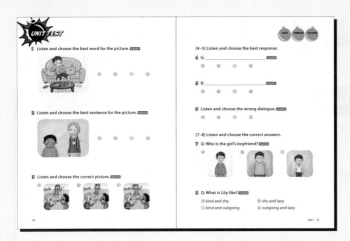

UNIT TEST

해당 Unit에서 배운 내용을 아우르는 다양한 유형의 실전 문제를 통해, 학습한 내용을 충실히 이해했는지 확인할 수 있습니다.

REVIEW TEST

3~4개의 Unit을 학습한 후, 총 10문항으로 구성된 누적 테스트를 풀어봄으로써 앞서 배운 내용에 대한 성취도를 확인할 수 있습니다.

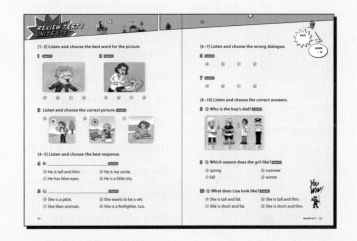

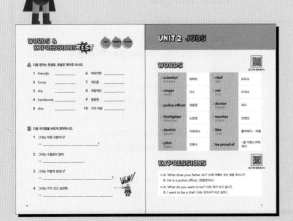

단어장

본책에서 학습한 단어와 표현이 보기 쉽게 정리되어 있습니다.
단어와 표현을 충분히 학습했는지 확인해 볼 수 있도록 간단한 테스트도 함께 제공됩니다.
단어와 표현에 대한 발음은 QR코드를 통해 손쉽게 확인 가능합니다.

★ OVERVIEW OF LISTENING BUDDY ★

Level	Unit	Title	Key Expressions	Key Words
Level 1	1	Greetings	Good morning. How are you? What's your name? This is my friend, Brian.	morning, afternoon, evening, name, friend, meet, nice
	2	My Family	Who is he? How old is she?	grandfather, grandmother, father, mother, brother, sister, uncle, aunt, cousin, twins
	3	Pets	Do you like birds? Do you have any pets?	dog, cat, rabbit, hamster, bird, fish, turtle, lizard
	4	Art Class	What is this/that? What are these/those? Is this/that your glue?	crayon, colored pencil, eraser, sketchbook, glue, scissors, ruler
	5	Music	Can you play the piano? What can you play?	piano, violin, cello, flute, guitar, drums, trumpet
	6	Yummy Food	Do you want some pizza? What do you want?	bread, sandwich, salad, pizza, chicken, noodles, fried rice
	7	Birthday Party	Happy birthday! This is for you. Thank you for coming. Would you like some cake?	card, cake, present, hairpin, robot, backpack, hat
	8	Outdoor Activities	Swim with your brother. Don't ride your bike here. Watch out! / Be careful!	swim, ride, catch, throw, climb up, push, wear
	9	Seven Days	What day is it today? What do you do on Sundays?	Sunday, Monday, Tuesday, Wednesday, Thursday, Friday, Saturday, play soccer, go hiking, have a yoga class, visit my uncle
	10	Weather	How's the weather? / What's the weather like? Let's play soccer outside.	sunny, cloudy, windy, rainy, snowy, hot, cold
Level 2	1	Colors and Shapes	What color is it? What shape is it?	red, yellow, green, blue, circle, square, rectangle, triangle
	2	Everyday Life	What time is it? What time do you go to bed?	get up, go to school, have lunch, go home, exercise, do homework, go to bed
	3	Feelings	How do you feel? Are you scared?	happy, sad, excited, angry, scared, bored, worried, tired
	4	Body Parts	What does it look like? How many eyes does it have?	eye, nose, mouth, ear, arm, hand, leg, foot

Level	Unit	Title	Key Expressions	Key Words
Level 2	5	At Home	Where is my car key? Whose socks are these?	key, watch, socks, glasses, bed, table, drawer, bookshelf
	6	School Subjects	What's your favorite subject? Are you interested in painting?	art, music, English, math, science, P.E., history
	7	Hobbies	What do you like to do in your free time? How about playing tennis after school?	listen to music, play tennis, watch movies, take photos, play computer games, do puzzles
	8	At the Festival	What are they doing? Can I drink some soda?	sing, dance on a stage, look for a restroom, eat snacks, drink soda, watch the fireworks
	9	Cooking	Will you wash the tomatoes? How does it taste?	wash, peel, mix, fry, sweet, salty, sour, spicy
	10	Shopping	I'm looking for a shirt. How much is this skirt? What size do you wear?	shirt, jacket, skirt, pants, shoes, gloves, umbrella
Level 3	1	People Around Me	What does she look like? What is she like?	tall, short, thin, fat, shy, outgoing, funny, lazy
	2	Jobs	What does your father do? What do you want to be?	scientist, singer, police officer, firefighter, dentist, pilot, chef, vet
	3	Four Seasons	Which seasons do you like? Why do you like summer?	spring, summer, fall, winter, go on a picnic, play at the beach, see colorful leaves, go skiing
	4	Sickness	I have a headache. You should see a doctor.	headache, toothache, stomachache, fever, cough, runny nose, sore throat, see a doctor, take medicine
	5	At the Restaurant	Are you ready to order? What would you like to have? May I have the bill, please?	order, menu, bill, dessert, steak, hamburger, French fries, pie
	6	Special Days	What's the date today? When is your birthday?	January, February, March, April, May, June, July, August, September, October, November, December, New Year's Day, Earth Day, Halloween, Christmas
	7	The Past	What did you do yesterday? How was your weekend?	played baseball, watched TV, visited a museum, went swimming, had a party, took a trip
	8	Phone Calls	May I speak to Amy? Who's calling, please? May I leave a message?	answer the phone, hold on, leave a message, call back, hang up, have the wrong number
	9	My Town	Where is the bakery? How can I get to the movie theater? Go straight and turn left.	library, bank, hospital, bakery, movie theater, turn left, turn right, go straight, next to, between
	10	Plans	What are you going to do tomorrow? Do you have any plans for your vacation?	go shopping, get a haircut, relax at home, go camping, study Chinese, travel overseas

★ CONTENTS ★

Let's meet our buddies in Listening Buddy!

Ann   Tom   Jack   Jenny   Kevin

UNIT 1
PEOPLE AROUND ME

ARE YOU READY?

⚡ Listen and number. `Track 001`

⭐ Listen and repeat. `Track 002`

tall

short

thin

fat

shy

outgoing

funny

lazy

START UP

A Listen and check. `Track 003`

1

2

3

B Listen and match. `Track 004`

1	**2**	**3**
Ben	Mike	Tim
•	•	•
•	•	•

SOUND SOUND

Listen and say. `Track 005`

/t/ tall time tree   /θ/ thin throw three

Listen and circle. `Track 006`

1 /t/ /θ/   **2** /t/ /θ/   **3** /t/ /θ/

LISTEN UP

A Listen and number. Track 007

B Listen and check. Track 008

1

2

3

4

C Listen and check. Track 009

TRUE FALSE

1 Tony is tall and thin.

2 The boy's cousin is kind and outgoing.

ⓓ Listen and choose. Track 010

1 Ted

ⓐ ⓑ ⓒ

2 Anna

ⓐ ⓑ ⓒ

LET'S SPEAK WITH BUDDY

Listen and say. Track 011

Do you know Jessica, the new student?

No, I don't.

What does she look like?

She is tall and pretty.

What is she like?

She's very kind and outgoing.

Oh, here she comes!

✛Listen again and repeat.

DICTATION

A **Listen and write the letters.** `Track 012`

1 ___at

2 sh___rt

3 ___ ___in

4 fu___ ___y

B **Listen and write the words.** `Track 013`

1 Is she _____?

2 Do you _____ Mrs. Brown?

3 He's very _____.

4 He is _____ and has big blue eyes.

5 What does your girlfriend _____ like?

C **Listen and fill in the blanks.**

1 `Track 014`

 : Do you know Kate? She's a new student.

: No. What does she _____ _____?

: She is _____ and has long hair.

2 `Track 015`

 : Who's that boy?

 : He's my new classmate, Ted.

: He's _____ and handsome!

: Yes, he is.

: _____ is he _____?

: He is a little _____.

3 `Track 016`

 : Do you _____ Tony?

 : No, I don't. Who is he?

: He is Peter's brother. He's _____ and
_____.

 : What does he look like?

 : He is handsome and has big blue eyes.

 : Is he tall?

 : No, he's _____ and thin.

UNIT TEST

1 Listen and choose the best word for the picture. `Track 017`

ⓐ   ⓑ   ⓒ   ⓓ

2 Listen and choose the best sentence for the picture. `Track 018`

ⓐ   ⓑ   ⓒ   ⓓ

3 Listen and choose the correct picture. `Track 019`

ⓐ    ⓑ    ⓒ

[4–5] Listen and choose the best response.

4 G: _____ `Track 020`

   ⓐ   ⓑ   ⓒ   ⓓ

5 B: _____ `Track 021`

   ⓐ   ⓑ   ⓒ   ⓓ

6 Listen and choose the wrong dialogue. `Track 022`

   ⓐ   ⓑ   ⓒ   ⓓ

[7–8] Listen and choose the correct answers.

7 Q: Who is the girl's boyfriend? `Track 023`

  ⓐ    ⓑ    ⓒ

8 Q: What is Lily like? `Track 024`

  ⓐ kind and shy   ⓑ shy and lazy

  ⓒ kind and outgoing   ⓓ outgoing and lazy

UNIT 2
JOBS

ARE YOU READY?

⚡ **Listen and number.** Track 025

☆ **Listen and repeat.** Track 026

scientist

singer

police officer

firefighter

dentist

pilot

chef

vet

START UP

A Listen and number. Track 027

☐ ☐ ☐ ☐

B Listen and match. Track 028

1   **2**   **3**

SOUND SOUND

Listen and say. Track 029

/ai/ scientist firefighter pilot life

● What does your father do?

● What do you want to be?

LISTEN UP

A Listen and match. Track 030

1	2	3
Joe	Mike	Lisa

• • •

• • •

| singer | vet | scientist |

B Listen and check. Track 031

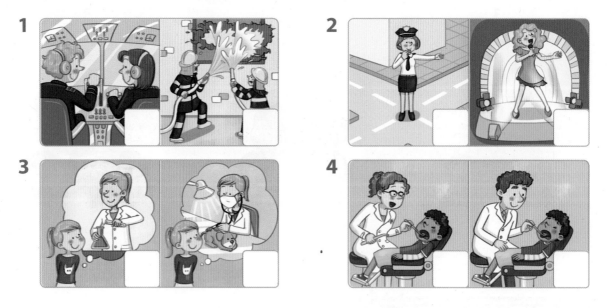

1

2

3

4

C Listen and check. Track 032

TRUE FALSE

1 The boy's brother wants to be a pilot.

2 The girl's mom is a chef.

ⓓ Listen and write. `Track 033`

My Dream

1 Luke ☐

2 Emma ☐

LET'S SPEAK WITH BUDDY

Listen and say. `Track 034`

What do you want to be in the future?

I want to be a vet.

I love animals.

How about you, Kevin?

I want to be Spider-Man. He is so cool.

✚ Listen again and repeat.

DICTATION

A Listen and write the letters. `Track 035`

1 p___lot

2 ___ ___ef

3 ___ ___ ___entist

4 pol___ ___ ___ officer

B Listen and write the words. `Track 036`

1 What do you _____ to be?

2 I want to be a _____ .

3 What does your mother _____ ?

4 Is your father a _____ ?

5 Do you want to be a _____ , too?

C Listen and fill in the blanks.

1 `Track 037`

 : Mike, what do you want to be?

 : I want to be a _____ .

My favorite subject is _____ .

2 `Track 038`

 : What do you _____ to be, Nick?

 : I want to be an English _____. I like English. How about you?

 : I want to be a _____. I like to cook.

 : Oh, really? My mom is a chef.

 : How wonderful!

3 `Track 039`

 : What does your father do?

 : He's a _____.

 : Do you want to be a pilot, too?

 : No, I want to be a _____ _____.

 : How about your brother? What does he want to be?

 : He wants to be a _____.

UNIT TEST

1 **Listen and choose the best word or phrase for the picture.** Track 040

ⓐ   ⓑ   ⓒ   ⓓ

2 **Listen and choose the best sentence for the picture.** Track 041

ⓐ   ⓑ   ⓒ   ⓓ

3 **Listen and choose the correct picture.** Track 042

ⓐ    ⓑ    ⓒ

[4–5] Listen and choose the best response.

4 B: _____ `Track 043`

ⓐ　　　ⓑ　　　ⓒ　　　ⓓ

5 G: _____ `Track 044`

ⓐ　　　ⓑ　　　ⓒ　　　ⓓ

6 Listen and choose the wrong dialogue. `Track 045`

ⓐ　　　ⓑ　　　ⓒ　　　ⓓ

[7–8] Listen and choose the correct answers.

7 Q: What does the boy's father do? `Track 046`

ⓐ  　　ⓑ  　　ⓒ

8 Q: What does the girl want to be? `Track 047`

ⓐ a chef　　　　　　ⓑ a vet

ⓒ a scientist　　　　ⓓ a firefighter

UNIT 3
FOUR SEASONS

ARE YOU READY?

⚡ **Listen and number.** Track 048

☆ **Listen and repeat.** Track 049

spring

summer

fall

winter

go on a picnic

play at the beach

see colorful leaves

go skiing

24

START UP

A Listen and number. `Track 050`

B Listen and match. `Track 051`

1 • 2 • 3 •

• • •

SOUND SOUND

Listen and say. `Track 052`

/sp/   spring   spider   speak   spend

• Which seasons do you like?

• Why do you like summer?

WoW!

LISTEN UP

A Listen and match. Track 053

1
Josh

2
Mary

3
Nick

•   •   •   •

spring   summer   fall   winter

B Listen and check. Track 054

1

2

3

4

C Listen and check. Track 055

	TRUE	FALSE
1 The girl likes summer and winter.		
2 The boy likes spring because he can go on a picnic.		

26

Ⓓ **Listen and write.** Track 056

1 Ted ☐

2 Joe ☐

LET'S SPEAK WITH BUDDY

Listen and say. Track 057

➕ Listen again and repeat.

DICTATION

A Listen and write the words. `Track 058`

1 go on a _____

2 see colorful _____

3 play at the _____

4 go _____

B Listen and write the words. `Track 059`

1 Which _____ do you like?

2 I like _____.

3 _____ do you like fall?

4 Because I can see _____ leaves.

5 Do you like _____?

C Listen and fill in the blanks.

1 `Track 060`

 : Which seasons do you like?

 : I like _____.

 : Why do you like it?

 : _____ I can eat lots of ice cream.

2 Track 061

: _____ _____ do you like?

: I like _____.

: Why do you like it?

: Because I like to _____ _____.
Do you like winter, too, Ted?

: No, I don't. I like summer.
I like to go _____.

3 Track 062

: Do you like _____?

: No, I don't.

: Then, which seasons do you like?

: I like _____ and summer.

: Why do you like spring and summer?

: Because I can _____ _____ a picnic in spring,
and I can _____ at the beach in summer.

UNIT TEST

1 Listen and choose the best word for the picture. `Track 063`

ⓐ   ⓑ   ⓒ   ⓓ

2 Listen and choose the best sentence for the picture. `Track 064`

ⓐ   ⓑ   ⓒ   ⓓ

3 Listen and choose the correct picture. `Track 065`

ⓐ    ⓑ    ⓒ

4 Listen and choose the best dialogue for the picture. Track 066

ⓐ   ⓑ   ⓒ   ⓓ

5 Listen and choose the best response. Track 067

G: _____

ⓐ   ⓑ   ⓒ   ⓓ

6 Listen and choose the wrong dialogue. Track 068

ⓐ   ⓑ   ⓒ   ⓓ

[7–8] Listen and choose the correct answers.

7 Q: Which season does the boy like? Track 069

ⓐ    ⓑ    ⓒ

8 Q: Why does the girl like summer? Track 070

ⓐ Because she likes to go hiking.

ⓑ Because she likes to go swimming.

ⓒ Because she likes to eat ice cream.

ⓓ Because she likes to play at the beach.

[1–2] Listen and choose the best word for the picture.

1 Track 071

ⓐ   ⓑ   ⓒ   ⓓ

2 Track 072

ⓐ   ⓑ   ⓒ   ⓓ

3 Listen and choose the correct picture. Track 073

ⓐ    ⓑ    ⓒ

[4–5] Listen and choose the best response.

4 B: _____ Track 074

ⓐ He is tall and thin.   ⓑ He is my uncle.

ⓒ He has blue eyes.   ⓓ He is a little shy.

5 G: _____ Track 075

ⓐ She is a pilot.   ⓑ She wants to be a vet.

ⓒ She likes animals.   ⓓ She is a firefighter, too.

[6–7] Listen and choose the wrong dialogue.

6 `Track 076`

ⓐ   ⓑ   ⓒ   ⓓ

7 `Track 077`

ⓐ   ⓑ   ⓒ   ⓓ

[8–10] Listen and choose the correct answers.

8 Q: Who is the boy's dad? `Track 078`

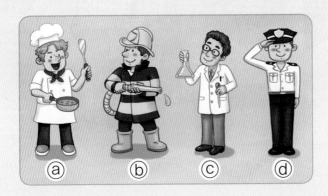

ⓐ   ⓑ   ⓒ   ⓓ

9 Q: Which season does the girl like? `Track 079`

ⓐ spring   ⓑ summer

ⓒ fall   ⓓ winter

10 Q: What does Lisa look like? `Track 080`

ⓐ She is tall and fat.   ⓑ She is tall and thin.

ⓒ She is short and fat.   ⓓ She is short and thin.

YOU WIN!

ARE YOU READY?

⚡ **Listen and number.** Track 081

☆ **Listen and repeat.** Track 082

headache toothache stomachache fever cough

runny nose sore throat see a doctor take medicine

A Listen and number. `Track 083`

B Listen and match. `Track 084`

1 •

2 •

3 •

• • •

SOUND SOUND

Listen and say. `Track 085`

/f/   cough   tough   enough   laugh

- I have a stomachache.
- We should see a doctor.

LISTEN UP

A Listen and number. `Track 086`

B Listen and check. `Track 087`

1

2

3

4

C Listen and check. `Track 088`

TRUE   **FALSE**

1 The girl has a fever and a cough.

2 The boy should see a doctor.

D Listen and mark. Track 089

	headache	toothache	fever	sore throat	runny nose
1					
2					
3					

LET'S SPEAK WITH BUDDY

Listen and say. Track 090

Jack, wake up!

Mom, should I go to school?

Why? What's wrong?

I have a headache.

Do you have a fever, too?

Yes, I do.

Let's see a doctor after school.

➕ Listen again and repeat.

DICTATION

A Listen and write the letters. `Track 091`

1 cou___ ___

2 t___ ___thache

3 medi___ ___ne

4 sore ___ ___roat

B Listen and write the words. `Track 092`

1 Are you okay? What's _____?

2 I have a _____.

3 You should see a _____.

4 Do you have a _____?

5 I have a _____.

C Listen and fill in the blanks.

1 `Track 093`

 : Are you okay? What's wrong?

: I have a _____.

: Oh, you should see a _____.

2 `Track 094`

 : Do you have a _____?

 : Yes, I do.

 : Maybe you should take some _____.

3 `Track 095`

 : Achoo!

 : Bless you! Do you have a _____?

 : Yes, I have a _____ and a _____.

 : Oh, you should rest at home.

4 `Track 096`

 : Are you okay? You don't look good.

 : I have a fever.

 : Do you have a _____ _____, too?

 : No, but I have a _____ _____.

 : Let's go to the doctor.

UNIT TEST

1 Listen and choose the best word or phrase for the picture. Track 097

ⓐ　　　ⓑ　　　ⓒ　　　ⓓ

2 Listen and choose the best sentence for the picture. Track 098

ⓐ　　　ⓑ　　　ⓒ　　　ⓓ

3 Listen and choose the correct picture. Track 099

ⓐ 　　ⓑ 　　ⓒ

[4–5] Listen and choose the best response.

4 B: _____ `Track 100`

    ⓐ   ⓑ   ⓒ   ⓓ

5 W: _____ `Track 101`

    ⓐ   ⓑ   ⓒ   ⓓ

6 Listen and choose the wrong dialogue. `Track 102`

    ⓐ   ⓑ   ⓒ   ⓓ

[7–8] Listen and choose the correct answers.

7 Q: What's wrong with the girl? `Track 103`

  ⓐ    ⓑ    ⓒ

8 Q: What should the boy do? `Track 104`

    ⓐ He should see a doctor.   ⓑ He should take medicine.
    ⓒ He should go to school.   ⓓ He should rest at home.

UNIT 5
AT THE RESTAURANT

ARE YOU READY?

⚡ **Listen and number.** Track 105

⭐ **Listen and repeat.** Track 106

order

menu

bill

dessert

steak

hamburger

French fries

pie

STARTS UP

A Listen and number. Track 107

B Listen and match. Track 108

1 **2** **3**

SOUND SOUND

Listen and say. Track 109

- Are you ready to order?
- What would you like to have?
- May I have the bill, please?

WoW!

LISTEN UP

A Listen and circle. Track 110

1

O	X

2

O	X

3

O	X

B Listen and check. Track 111

1

2

3

4

C Listen and check. Track 112

	TRUE	FALSE
1 The man will have the cheesecake.		
2 The girl doesn't want an orange juice.		

D Listen and mark. `Track 113`

1

Order

- Cheesecake ☐
- Milk ☐
- Apple pie ☐
- Lemonade ☐
- Ice cream ☐

2

Order

- Steak ☐
- Soda ☐
- Hamburger ☐
- Orange juice ☐
- Chicken ☐

LET'S SPEAK WITH BUDDY

Listen and say. `Track 114`

I'm hungry.

Let's go there!

What would you like to have?

I want a hamburger and a soda.

Are you ready to order?

Yes, we want two hamburgers and two sodas, please.

Sorry, but we only have desserts.

MENU

➕ Listen again and repeat.

DICTATION

A **Listen and write the letters.** Track 115

1 m___n___

2 st___ ___k

3 de___ ___ert

4 ham___ ___ ___ger

B **Listen and write the words.** Track 116

1 Are you ready to _____?

2 I'll have the apple _____.

3 What would you _____ to have?

4 Anything to _____?

5 May I have the _____, please?

C **Listen and fill in the blanks.**

1 Track 117

 : Are you _____ to order?

 : Yes. I'll have a hamburger and _____ _____.

 : Anything to drink?

 : Soda, please.

2   Track 118

 : Josh, what _____ you _____ to have?

 : I'm still thinking. How about you?

 : I'll have the _____.

 : Okay. I'll have the chicken.

 : Good. Anything to drink?

 : I'll have a _____.

3   Track 119

 : Excuse me.

 : Yes, sir. Can I help you?

 : May I have the _____ _____?

 : Sure. Here you are.

 : Oh, this cheesecake looks delicious. I'll _____ that.

 : Okay. _____ else?

 : No, that's all. Thank you.

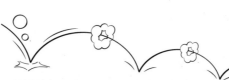

UNIT TEST

1 **Listen and choose the best word or phrase for the picture.** Track 120

ⓐ ⓑ ⓒ ⓓ

2 **Look, listen, and choose the answer.** Track 121

ⓐ ⓑ ⓒ ⓓ

3 **Listen and choose the correct picture.** Track 122

ⓐ    ⓑ    ⓒ

[4–5] Listen and choose the best response.

4 G: _____ Track 123

    ⓐ   ⓑ   ⓒ   ⓓ

5 M: _____ Track 124

    ⓐ   ⓑ   ⓒ   ⓓ

6 Listen and choose the wrong dialogue. Track 125

    ⓐ   ⓑ   ⓒ   ⓓ

[7–8] Listen and choose the correct answers.

7 Q: What will the woman do next? Track 126

ⓐ    ⓑ    ⓒ

8 Q: What would the girl like to have? Track 127

  ⓐ a hamburger   ⓑ a hamburger and a soda

  ⓒ a steak and a soda   ⓓ a steak and a salad

UNIT 6
SPECIAL DAYS

ARE YOU READY?

⚡ Listen and number. `Track 128`

☆ Listen and repeat. `Track 129`

January	February	March	April	May	June

July	August	September	October	November	December

New Year's Day
January 1

Earth Day
April 22

Halloween
October 31

Christmas
December 25

50

A Listen and number. `Track 130`

B Listen and match. `Track 131`

1

2

3

SOUND SOUND

Listen and say. `Track 132`

/st/ August first best past

● What's the date today? ⤵

● When is your birthday? ⤵

LISTEN UP

A Listen and circle. Track 133

1 July

WED	THU	FRI	SAT
1	Amy's birthday		④
8			

O   X

2 February

TUE	WED	THU	FRI	
3	4	5	6	
10	⑪ singing contest			

O   X

3 Octorber

ON	TUE	WED	THU	FR
			1	2
5	⑥ school festival			9
12	13	14	15	16

O   X

B Listen and check. Track 134

1

2

3

4

C Listen and check. Track 135

	TRUE	FALSE
1 Today is September 2.	☐	☐
2 The boy's birthday is May 7.	☐	☐

D Listen and write. Track 136

ⓐ

ⓑ

Our Plans

ⓒ

ⓓ

1 _____

2 _____

LET'S SPEAK WITH BUDDY

Listen and say. Track 137

What's the date today?

It's June 1.

Today is Jenny's birthday! Let's have a surprise party for her.

Happy birthday, Jenny!

What? Today isn't my birthday.

When is your birthday?

It's July 1.

✤ Listen again and repeat.

DICTATION

A Listen and write the letters. `Track 138`

1 Ju___ ___

2 Ja___ ___ ___ry

3 Augu___ ___

4 No___ ___ ___ber

B Listen and write the words. `Track 139`

1 What's the _____ today?

2 My _____ is next week.

3 Is today _____ 1?

4 _____ is Halloween?

5 Today is _____ 14.

C Listen and fill in the blanks.

1 `Track 140`

 : Amy, _____ is your birthday?

 : It's _____ 4.

 : Oh, it's tomorrow!

2 Track 141

 : When is your school _____?

 : It's next week, _____ 16. Can you come?

 : Sure.

3 Track 142

 : What's the date today?

 : It's _____ 22.

 : Oh, it's _____ _____. Let's pick up trash.

 : That's a good idea.

4 Track 143

 : _____ is next week!

 : Oh, really? What's the date today?

 : It's _____ 21.

 : Do you have any special _____ for Christmas?

 : Yes. I'll visit my grandmother.

UNIT TEST

1 Listen and choose the best word or phrase for the picture. Track 144

ⓐ   ⓑ   ⓒ   ⓓ

2 Listen and choose the best sentence for the picture. Track 145

ⓐ   ⓑ   ⓒ   ⓓ

3 Listen and choose the correct picture. Track 146

ⓐ    ⓑ    ⓒ

4 Listen and choose the best dialogue for the picture. Track 147

ⓐ   ⓑ   ⓒ   ⓓ

5 Listen and choose the best response. Track 148

ⓐ   ⓑ   ⓒ   ⓓ

6 Listen and choose the wrong dialogue. Track 149

ⓐ   ⓑ   ⓒ   ⓓ

[7–8] Listen and choose the correct answers.

7 Q: When is Dad's birthday? Track 150

ⓐ March   ⓑ March   ⓒ March

8 Q: Today is _____. Track 151

ⓐ December 20   ⓑ December 21

ⓒ December 24   ⓓ December 25

[1–2] Listen and choose the best word or phrase for the picture.

1 `Track 152`

2 `Track 153`

ⓐ   ⓑ   ⓒ   ⓓ

ⓐ   ⓑ   ⓒ   ⓓ

3 Listen and choose the correct picture. `Track 154`

ⓐ   ⓑ   ⓒ

[4–5] Listen and choose the best response.

4 B: _____ `Track 155`

   ⓐ It's July 4.   ⓑ It's July 9.

   ⓒ Let's throw a party.   ⓓ It's Amy's birthday.

5 G: _____ `Track 156`

   ⓐ Let's go to the dentist.   ⓑ Should I go to the doctor?

   ⓒ You should take medicine.   ⓓ I have a runny nose, too.

[6–7] Listen and choose the wrong dialogue.

6 `Track 157`

ⓐ   ⓑ   ⓒ   ⓓ

7 `Track 158`

ⓐ   ⓑ   ⓒ   ⓓ

[8–10] Listen and choose the correct answers.

8 Q: Which one is the boy's food? `Track 159`

9 Q: What is the date today? `Track 160`

ⓐ September 18   ⓑ September 19

ⓒ September 25   ⓓ September 26

10 Q: The girl has _____. `Track 161`

ⓐ a cough   ⓑ a fever and a cough

ⓒ a cough and a headache   ⓓ a fever and a headache

UNIT 7
THE PAST

ARE YOU READY?

⚡ **Listen and number.** Track 162

☆ **Listen and repeat.** Track 163

played baseball

watched TV

visited a museum

went swimming

had a party

took a trip

60

A Listen and number. Track 164

☐ ☐ ☐

B Listen and match. Track 165

1 • 2 • 3 •

• • •

SOUND SOUND

Listen and say. Track 166

/d/ played cleaned called   /t/ watched jumped walked

Listen and circle. Track 167

1 /d/ /t/   **2** /d/ /t/   **3** /d/ /t/

LISTEN UP

A Listen and match. Track 168

1	2	3
Kate	Dan	Mary

•   •   •

•   •   •

played tennis	watched a baseball game	had a party

B Listen and check. Track 169

C Listen and check. Track 170

                                                                TRUE   FALSE

1 The girl didn't visit a museum yesterday. ☐ ☐

2 The boy watched TV at home last weekend. ☐ ☐

ⓓ **Listen and number in time order.** Track 171

1   2   3

☐ → ☐ → ☐

LET'S SPEAK WITH BUDDY

Listen and say. Track 172

♦Listen again and repeat.

DICTATION

A **Listen and write the words.** `Track 173`

1 _____ a party

2 _____ TV

3 _____ a trip

4 _____ baseball

B **Listen and write the words.** `Track 174`

1 What did you _____ yesterday?

2 How _____ your trip?

3 I _____ a lot of museums.

4 I _____ swimming with my father.

5 _____ you play baseball last weekend?

C **Listen and fill in the blanks.**

1 `Track 175`

 : Did you _____ to a movie yesterday?

 : No, I didn't. I just _____ TV at home.

2 `Track 176`

 : Did you go to Sam's birthday party?

 : Yes, I did. I _____ see you there.

 : I was busy yesterday.

 : What did you do?

 : I _____ a museum.

 : _____ you have fun?

 : Yes, I did. I _____ a lot of photos.

3 `Track 177`

 : _____ _____ your weekend?

 : It was great. I was at my uncle's house.

 : What did you do there?

 : I _____ swimming with my cousins on Saturday.

 : What about on Sunday?

 : We _____ baseball in the morning and then we

_____ lunch together.

UNIT TEST

1 Listen and choose the best phrase for the picture. Track 178

ⓐ　　　ⓑ　　　ⓒ　　　ⓓ

2 Listen and choose the best sentence for the picture. Track 179

ⓐ　　　ⓑ　　　ⓒ　　　ⓓ

3 Listen and choose the correct picture. Track 180

ⓐ 　　ⓑ 　　ⓒ

[4–5] Listen and choose the best response.

4 G: _____ Track 181

ⓐ   ⓑ   ⓒ   ⓓ

5 B: _____ Track 182

ⓐ   ⓑ   ⓒ   ⓓ

6 Listen and choose the wrong dialogue. Track 183

ⓐ   ⓑ   ⓒ   ⓓ

[7–8] Listen and choose the correct answers.

7 Q: What did the girl do yesterday? Track 184

ⓐ    ⓑ    ⓒ

8 Q: The boy _____ last weekend. Track 185

ⓐ went swimming   ⓑ had a party

ⓒ visited a museum   ⓓ played baseball

UNIT 8
PHONE CALLS

ARE YOU READY?

⚡ **Listen and number.** `Track 186`

⭐ **Listen and repeat.** `Track 187`

answer the phone

hold on

leave a message

call back

hang up

have the wrong number

START UP

A Listen and number. `Track 188`

B Listen and match. `Track 189`

1 •

2 •

3 •

•

•

•

SOUND SOUND

Listen and say. `Track 190`

/f/ phone photo dolphin elephant

● May I speak to Amy?↗

● May I leave a message?↗

LISTEN UP

A Listen and match. `Track 191`

1	2	3
From: Sue	From: Mark	From: Julie
•	•	•
•	•	•
Meet at 3	Call back at 7	Meet at the park

B Listen and check. `Track 192`

1 **2** **3** **4**

324 – 3562?

C Listen and check. `Track 193`

TRUE   FALSE

1 The girl will call back at 5.

2 The boy will go to the movie tomorrow.

D Listen and number in order. Track 194

1   2   3

☐ → ☐ → ☐

LET'S SPEAK WITH BUDDY

Listen and say. Track 195

✚ Listen again and repeat.

DICTATION

A Listen and write the words. Track 196

1 call _____

2 _____ up

3 _____ on

4 _____ the phone

B Listen and write the words. Track 197

1 May I _____ to Amy?

2 You have the _____ number.

3 I can't answer the _____ right now.

4 May I leave a _____?

5 Please tell her to _____ me back.

C Listen and fill in the blanks.

1 Track 198

: May I speak to Josh?

: _____. Who's _____, please?

: This is Sue.

2 `Track 199`

 : This is Julie. _____ I _____ a message?

 : Sure.

 : Please tell Peter to _____ me at 3, not 2.

3 `Track 200`

 : _____ _____ Jessica. I can't answer the phone right now. Please leave a message.

 : Hi, Jessica. This is Kevin. Please _____ me _____ after school.

4 `Track 201`

 : Hello? May I _____ to Ben?

 : My brother is not at home right now.

 : Okay. I'll call him back.

 : Oh, don't _____ _____. He's home now. _____ _____, please.

UNIT TEST

1 Listen and choose the best phrase for the picture. `Track 202`

ⓐ　　　ⓑ　　　ⓒ　　　ⓓ

2 Listen and choose the correct picture. `Track 203`

ⓐ 　　ⓑ 　　ⓒ

3 Listen and choose the best dialogue for the picture. `Track 204`

ⓐ　　　ⓑ　　　ⓒ　　　ⓓ

[4–5] Listen and choose the best response.

4 G: _____ `Track 205`

ⓐ   ⓑ   ⓒ   ⓓ

5 B: _____ `Track 206`

ⓐ   ⓑ   ⓒ   ⓓ

6 Listen and choose the wrong dialogue. `Track 207`

ⓐ   ⓑ   ⓒ   ⓓ

[7–8] Listen and choose the correct answers.

7 Q: Which one is the correct message? `Track 208`

ⓐ From: Kelly Meet at 6   ⓑ From: John Meet at 6   ⓒ From: Kelly Meet at 4

8 Q: What will the boy do next? `Track 209`

ⓐ He will leave a message.

ⓑ He will hang up the phone.

ⓒ He will call Anna back.

ⓓ He will talk to Anna on the phone.

UNIT 9
MY TOWN

ARE YOU READY?

⚡ **Listen and number.** `Track 210`

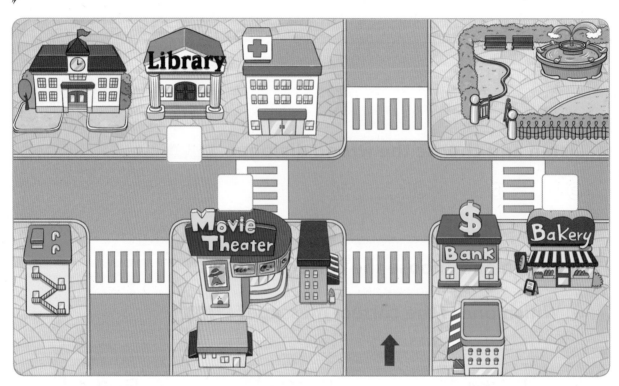

☆ **Listen and repeat.** `Track 211`

library

bank

hospital

bakery

movie theater

turn left

turn right

go straight

next to

between

76

START UP

A Listen and number. `Track 212`

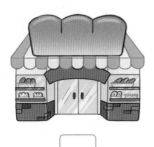

B Listen and match. `Track 213`

1   **2**   **3**

SOUND SOUND

Listen and say. `Track 214`

/əː/   turn   learn   nurse   Earth

- Where is the library?
- Go straight and turn left.

LISTEN UP

A Listen and match. `Track 215`

1	2	3
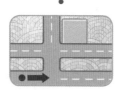		

•   •   •

•   •   •

B Listen and write the numbers. `Track 216`

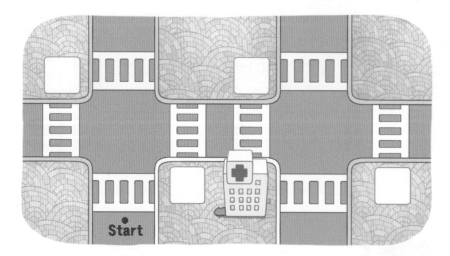

Start

C Listen and check. `Track 217`

1 The woman will go straight and turn left. ☐ ☐

2 The hospital is between the park and the school. ☐ ☐

⒟ Listen and write. Track 218

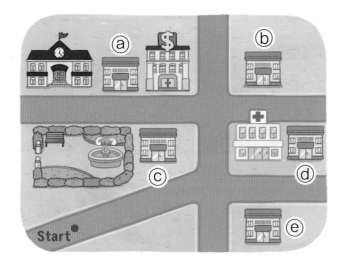

Find the buildings.

1 _____

2 _____

3 _____

LET'S SPEAK WITH BUDDY

Listen and say. Track 219

✚ Listen again and repeat.

DICTATION

A **Listen and write the words.** `Track 220`

1 _____

2 turn _____

3 movie _____

4 turn _____

B **Listen and write the words.** `Track 221`

1 Go _____ and turn left.

2 It's _____ _____ the library.

3 Is there a _____ around here?

4 How can I _____ _____ the hospital?

5 It's _____ the park and the school.

C **Listen and fill in the blanks.**

1 `Track 222`

: Excuse me. Where is the _____?

: Go straight and turn _____. It will be on your left.

: Okay. Thank you for your help.

2 `Track 223`

 : Excuse me. Is _____ a park around here?

 : Yes, there is.

 : How can I _____ there?

 : Go straight and _____ _____. It will be on your right. Do you understand?

 : Yes. Thank you very much.

3 `Track 224`

 : Excuse me. How can I get to the _____ from here?

 : Pardon?

 : How can I get to the hospital from here?

 : _____ _____ and turn right.
It's _____ the school and the bank.

 : Oh, I see. Thank you.

 : You're welcome.

UNIT TEST

1 **Listen and choose the best word for the picture.** Track 225

ⓐ　　　ⓑ　　　ⓒ　　　ⓓ

2 **Listen and choose the best sentence for the picture.** Track 226

ⓐ　　　ⓑ　　　ⓒ　　　ⓓ

3 **Listen and choose the correct picture.** Track 227

ⓐ 　　ⓑ 　　ⓒ

[4–5] **Listen and choose the best response.**

4 **G:** _____ Track 228

ⓐ   ⓑ   ⓒ   ⓓ

5 **W:** _____ Track 229

ⓐ   ⓑ   ⓒ   ⓓ

6 **Listen and choose the wrong dialogue.** Track 230

ⓐ   ⓑ   ⓒ   ⓓ

[7–8] **Listen and choose the correct answers.**

7 **Q: Where is the hospital?** Track 231

ⓐ 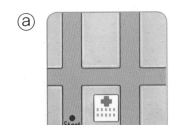   ⓑ 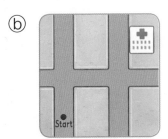   ⓒ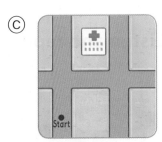

8 **Q: The boy will go straight, _____.** Track 232

ⓐ and turn right   ⓑ turn left, and turn right

ⓒ turn right, and turn left   ⓓ turn left, and turn left again

UNIT 10 PLANS

ARE YOU READY?

⚡ **Listen and number.** Track 233

☆ **Listen and repeat.** Track 234

go shopping

get a haircut

relax at home

go camping

study Chinese

travel overseas

A Listen and number. Track 235

B Listen and match. Track 236

1 •   2 •   3 •

•   •   •

SOUND SOUND

Listen and say. Track 237

/i/ relax review become before

○ What are you going to do tomorrow?

○ Do you have any plans for your vacation?

WoW!

LISTEN UP

A Listen and match. Track 238

1	2	3
Peter	Amy	Lisa

• • •

• • •

go camping   get a haircut   study Chinese

B Listen and check. Track 239

1

2

3

4

C Listen and check. Track 240

TRUE   FALSE

1 The boy is going to go skiing for vacation.

2 The girl is going to get a haircut tomorrow.

D Listen and write. `Track 241`

ⓐ

ⓑ

Vacation Plan

1 Sam ☐

ⓒ Chinese

ⓓ

2 Lily ☐

LET'S SPEAK WITH BUDDY

Listen and say. `Track 242`

➕ Listen again and repeat.

DICTATION

A **Listen and write the words.** Track 243

1 _____ overseas

2 go _____

3 get a _____

4 _____ Chinese

B **Listen and write the words.** Track 244

1 What are you _____ to do this weekend?

2 I'm going to go _____.

3 Do you have any _____ for your vacation?

4 Are you going to _____ at home?

5 I'm going to travel _____ with my family.

C **Listen and fill in the blanks.**

1 Track 245

: Peter, what are you going to do _____?

: I'm going to study _____.
I have a test next week.

2 `Track 246`

    : Lisa, what are you going to do this _____?

    : I'm going to go _____. I'm so excited.

    : That sounds fun!

3 `Track 247`

    : Do you have any plans for this Sunday?

    : Yes, I'm going to _____ _____.
      How about you?

    : I'm going to _____ a _____.
      I want a new style.

4 `Track 248`

    : Do you have any plans for your _____?

    : Yes, I'm going to _____ to Europe.

    : Cool! What are you going to do there?

    : I'm going to _____ museums. How about you?

    : I'm going to _____ _____ with my family.

    : Oh, that sounds exciting. Have fun!

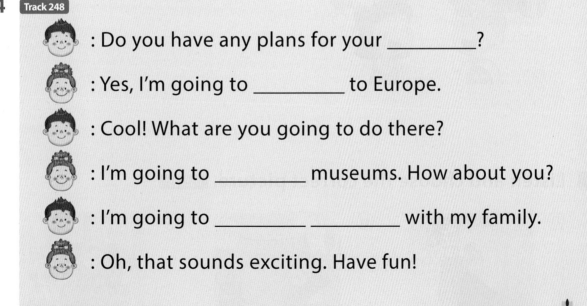

1 Listen and choose the best phrase for the picture. Track 249

ⓐ   ⓑ   ⓒ   ⓓ

2 Listen and choose the best sentence for the picture. Track 250

ⓐ   ⓑ   ⓒ   ⓓ

3 Listen and choose the correct picture. Track 251

ⓐ    ⓑ    ⓒ

[4–5] Listen and choose the best response.

4 B: _____ `Track 252`

    ⓐ   ⓑ   ⓒ   ⓓ

5 G: _____ `Track 253`

    ⓐ   ⓑ   ⓒ   ⓓ

6 Listen and choose the wrong dialogue. `Track 254`

    ⓐ   ⓑ   ⓒ   ⓓ

[7–8] Listen and choose the correct answers.

7 Q: What is the girl going to do tomorrow? `Track 255`

   ⓐ    ⓑ    ⓒ

8 Q: The boy is going to _____ this weekend. `Track 256`

   ⓐ get a haircut   ⓑ relax at home

   ⓒ travel overseas   ⓓ go camping

[1–2] Listen and choose the best phrase for the picture.

1 `Track 257`

ⓐ   ⓑ   ⓒ   ⓓ

2 `Track 258`

ⓐ   ⓑ   ⓒ   ⓓ

3 Listen and choose the correct picture. `Track 259`

ⓐ    ⓑ    ⓒ

[4–5] Listen and choose the best response.

4 M: _____ `Track 260`

ⓐ Oh, I see. Thank you.   ⓑ That's right. It will be on your right.

ⓒ Sure. My pleasure.   ⓓ Pardon? Could you tell me again?

5 G: _____ `Track 261`

ⓐ Sorry, I'm so tired.   ⓑ Yes. Can I go with you?

ⓒ That sounds fun!   ⓓ Yes, I'm going to get a haircut.

[6–7] Listen and choose the wrong dialogue.

6 `Track 262`

ⓐ ⓑ ⓒ ⓓ

7 `Track 263`

ⓐ ⓑ ⓒ ⓓ

[8–10] Listen and choose the correct answers.

8 Q: Where is the hospital? `Track 264`

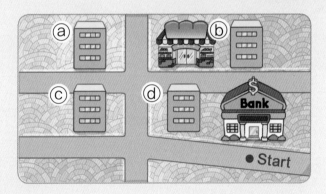

9 Q: What will the girl do next? `Track 265`

ⓐ She will call Nick back. ⓑ She will answer the phone.

ⓒ She will leave a message. ⓓ She will talk to Nick on the phone.

10 Q: The boy is going to _____ for vacation. `Track 266`

ⓐ go camping ⓑ relax at home

ⓒ study Chinese ⓓ travel overseas

지은이

NE능률 영어교육연구소

NE능률 영어교육연구소는 혁신적이며 효율적인 영어 교재를 개발하고
영어 학습의 질을 한 단계 높이고자 노력하는 NE능률의 연구조직입니다.

리스닝버디 3

펴 낸 이	주민홍
펴 낸 곳	서울특별시 마포구 월드컵북로 396(상암동) 누리꿈스퀘어 비즈니스타워 10층
	(주)NE능률 (우편번호 03925)
펴 낸 날	2016년 1월 5일 개정판 제1쇄
	2021년 10월 15일 제9쇄
전 화	02 2014 7114
팩 스	02 3142 0356
홈 페 이 지	www.neungyule.com
등 록 번 호	제 1-68호
I S B N	979-11-253-0974-1 63740
정 가	13,000원

NE 능률

고객센터

교재 내용 문의 : contact.nebooks.co.kr (별도의 가입 절차 없이 작성 가능)
제품 구매, 교환, 불량, 반품 문의 : 02-2014-7114
☎ 전화문의는 본사 업무시간 중에만 가능합니다.

NE능률 교재 MAP

아래 교재 MAP을 참고하여 본인의 현재 혹은 목표 수준에 따라 교재를 선택하세요.
NE능률 교재들과 함께 영어실력을 쑥쑥~ 올려보세요!
MP3 등 교재 부가 학습 서비스 및 자세한 교재 정보는 www.nebooks.co.kr 에서 확인하세요.

듣기
말하기
쓰기

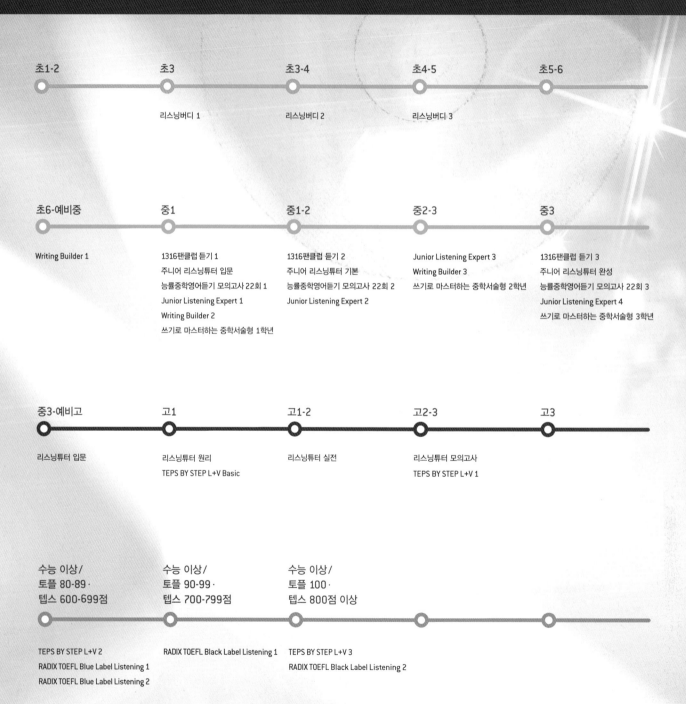

초1-2	초3	초3-4	초4-5	초5-6
	리스닝버디 1	리스닝버디 2	리스닝버디 3	

초6-예비중	중1	중1-2	중2-3	중3
Writing Builder 1	1316팬클럽 듣기 1	1316팬클럽 듣기 2	Junior Listening Expert 3	1316팬클럽 듣기 3
	주니어 리스닝튜터 입문	주니어 리스닝튜터 기본	Writing Builder 3	주니어 리스닝튜터 완성
	능률중학영어듣기 모의고사 22회 1	능률중학영어듣기 모의고사 22회 2	쓰기로 마스터하는 중학서술형 2학년	능률중학영어듣기 모의고사 22회 3
	Junior Listening Expert 1	Junior Listening Expert 2		Junior Listening Expert 4
	Writing Builder 2			쓰기로 마스터하는 중학서술형 3학년
	쓰기로 마스터하는 중학서술형 1학년			

중3-예비고	고1	고1-2	고2-3	고3
리스닝튜터 입문	리스닝튜터 원리	리스닝튜터 실전	리스닝튜터 모의고사	
	TEPS BY STEP L+V Basic		TEPS BY STEP L+V 1	

수능 이상/ 토플 80-89· 텝스 600-699점	수능 이상/ 토플 90-99· 텝스 700-799점	수능 이상/ 토플 100· 텝스 800점 이상		
TEPS BY STEP L+V 2	RADIX TOEFL Black Label Listening 1	TEPS BY STEP L+V 3		
RADIX TOEFL Blue Label Listening 1		RADIX TOEFL Black Label Listening 2		
RADIX TOEFL Blue Label Listening 2				

초등학생의 영어 친구

리스닝 버디

정답 및 해석

3

NE 능률

초등학생의 영어 친구

리스닝 버디

정답 및 해석

3

UNIT 1 PEOPLE AROUND ME

ANSWERS

P.8

UNIT 1 PEOPLE AROUND ME

ARE YOU READY?

🔆 Listen and number.

★ Listen and repeat.

tall   short   thin   fat

shy   outgoing   funny   lazy

8

P.9

START UP

A Listen and check.
1 ✓ 2 ✓ 3 ✓

B Listen and match.
1 Ben   2 Mike   3 Tim

SOUND SOUND

🔊 Listen and say.
/t/ tall time tree   /θ/ thin throw three

🔊 Listen and circle.
1 /t/ (/θ/)   2 (/t/) /θ/   3 /t/ (/θ/)

UNIT 1   9

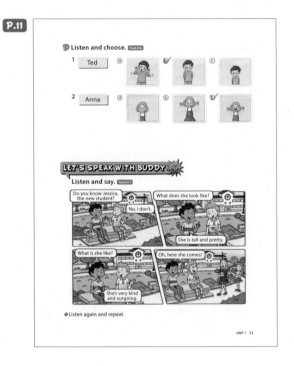

P.10

LISTEN UP

A Listen and number.
2   3   1

B Listen and check.
1 ✓ 2 ✓ 3 ✓ 4 ✓

C Listen and check.

	TRUE	FALSE
1 Tony is tall and thin.		✓
2 The boy's cousin is kind and outgoing.	✓	

10

P.11

D Listen and choose.
1 Ted   ⓑ
2 Anna   ©

LET'S SPEAK WITH BUDDY

Listen and say.

Do you know Jessica, the new student?
No, I don't.
What does she look like?
She is tall and pretty.
What is she like?
She's very kind and outgoing.
Oh, here she comes!

❖Listen again and repeat.

UNIT 1   11

P.12~13 **DICTATION**

A 1 f   2 o   3 t, h   4 n, n

B 1 outgoing   2 know   3 lazy
4 tall   5 look

2

C 1 look, like, thin
  2 tall, What, like, shy
  3 know, outgoing, funny, short

P.14~15 **UNIT TEST**

  1 ⓒ 2 ⓓ 3 ⓑ 4 ⓓ
  5 ⓒ 6 ⓓ 7 ⓐ 8 ⓒ

SCRIPTS & 해석

P.8 **ARE YOU READY?**

⚡ **Listen and number.**
  1 **G**: What does your girlfriend look like?
    (네 여자친구는 어떻게 생겼니?)
    B: She is tall and thin. (그녀는 키가 크고 날씬해.)

  2 **B**: That's my sister, Angela.
    (저 애는 내 여동생 Angela야.)
    G: She's cute. What is she like?
    (귀엽다. 그녀는 어떤 사람이니?)
    B: She is shy. (그녀는 수줍음이 많아.)

⭐ **Listen and repeat.**
  tall (키가 큰)   short (키가 작은)
  thin (날씬한)   fat (뚱뚱한)
  shy (수줍음을 많이 타는)   outgoing (외향적인)
  funny (재미있는)   lazy (게으른)

P.9 **START UP**

Ⓐ **Listen and check.**
  1 fat (뚱뚱한)
  2 funny (재미있는)
  3 short (키가 작은)

Ⓑ **Listen and match.**
  1 **B**: What is Ben like? (Ben은 어떤 사람이니?)
    G: He is lazy. (그는 게을러.)

  2 **B**: What does Mike look like?
    (Mike는 어떻게 생겼니?)
    G: He is thin. (그는 날씬해.)

  3 **B**: Is Tim shy? (Tim은 수줍음이 많니?)
    G: No, he isn't. He's outgoing.
    (아니, 그렇지 않아. 그는 외향적이야.)

P.9 **SOUND SOUND**

⬡ **Listen and say.**
  /t/ tall (키가 큰)   time (시간)   tree (나무)
  /θ/ thin (날씬한)   throw (던지다) three (3, 셋)

✚ **Listen and circle.**
  1 thin   2 time   3 three

P.10~11 **LISTEN UP**

Ⓐ **Listen and number.**
  1 **G**: Do you know Kate? She's a new student.
    (너 Kate를 아니? 그녀는 새로운 학생이야.)
    B: No. What does she look like?
    (아니. 그녀는 어떻게 생겼니?)
    G: She is thin and has long hair.
    (그녀는 날씬하고 머리가 길어.)

  2 **G**: That's my friend, Sue. (저 애는 내 친구 Sue야.)
    B: She's cute! What is she like?
    (귀엽다! 그녀는 어떤 사람이니?)
    G: She is outgoing and funny.
    (그녀는 외향적이고 재미있어.)

  3 **G**: Do you have a girlfriend?
    (너는 여자친구가 있니?)
    B: Yes, I do. (응, 있어.)
    G: What does she look like?
    (그녀는 어떻게 생겼니?)
    B: She's tall and has red hair.
    (그녀는 키가 크고 머리는 빨간색이야.)

Ⓑ **Listen and check.**
  1 **B**: Who's that girl? (저 소녀는 누구니?)
    G: She's a new student. (그녀는 새로운 학생이야.)
    B: What is she like? Is she outgoing?
    (그녀는 어떤 사람이니? 외향적이니?)
    G: No, she's a little shy.
    (아니, 그녀는 약간 수줍음이 많아.)

  2 **G**: Do you know Mrs. Brown?
    (너 Brown 선생님을 아니?)
    B: No. Who is she? (아니. 그녀는 누구니?)
    G: She's my English teacher. She's friendly.
    (그녀는 우리 영어 선생님이셔. 친절하셔.)
    B: What does she look like? Is she tall?
    (선생님은 어떻게 생기셨니? 키가 크시니?)
    G: No, she's short and a little fat.
    (아니, 선생님은 키가 작고 좀 뚱뚱하셔.)

  3 **G**: Who is he? (그는 누구니?)
    B: He's my uncle. (그는 우리 삼촌이셔.)

G: He looks nice. What is he like?
(멋져 보이신다. 삼촌은 어떤 분이니?)
B: He's very lazy. (삼촌은 매우 게으르셔.)

4 **G**: Do you know Josh? (너 Josh를 아니?)
B: No, I don't. (아니, 몰라.)
G: He is Peter's brother.
(그는 Peter의 남동생이야.)
B: What does he look like? (그는 어떻게 생겼니?)
G: He is tall and handsome.
(그는 키가 크고 잘생겼어.)

C Listen and check.

1 **G**: Do you know Tony? (너 Tony를 아니?)
B: No, I don't. Who is he? (아니, 몰라. 그는 누구니?)
G: He's a new student. He's very friendly.
(그는 새로운 학생이야. 그는 매우 친절해.)
B: What does he look like? (그는 어떻게 생겼니?)
G: He is handsome and has big blue eyes.
(그는 잘생겼고 눈이 크고 파란색이야.)
B: Is he tall? (그는 키가 크니?)
G: No, he's short and thin.
(아니, 그는 키가 작고 날씬해.)

Question: Tony is tall and thin.
(Tony는 키가 크고 날씬하다.)

2 **G**: Who's that girl over there?
(저기 저 소녀는 누구니?)
B: Oh, that's my cousin. (오, 저 애는 내 사촌이야.)
G: She is cute. (귀엽다.)
B: Yes, she is. (응, 맞아.)
G: What is she like? (그녀는 어떤 사람이니?)
B: She's very kind and outgoing.
(그녀는 매우 친절하고 외향적이야.)

Question: The boy's cousin is kind and
outgoing.
(소년의 사촌은 친절하고 외향적이다.)

D Listen and choose.

1 **G**: Who's that boy? (저 소년은 누구니?)
B: He's my new classmate, Ted.
(그는 내 새로운 반 친구인 Ted야.)
G: He's tall and handsome!
(그는 키가 크고 잘생겼구나!)
B: Yes, he is. (응, 맞아.)
G: What is he like? (그는 어떤 사람이니?)
B: He is a little shy. (그는 약간 수줍음이 많아.)

2 **G**: Do you know Anna? (너 Anna를 아니?)
B: No, I don't. Who is Anna?
(아니, 몰라. Anna가 누구니?)

G: She is Mary's sister. (그녀는 Mary의 언니야.)
B: Oh, what does she look like? Is she tall?
(오, 그녀는 어떻게 생겼니? 키가 크니?)
G: No, she isn't. But she is thin and pretty.
(아니, 크지 않아. 하지만 그녀는 날씬하고 예뻐.)
B: What is she like? (그녀는 어떤 사람이니?)
G: She's outgoing and funny.
(그녀는 외향적이고 재미있어.)

P.11 LET'S SPEAK WITH BUDDY

Listen and say.

Tom: Do you know Jessica, the new student?
(너 새로운 학생인 Jessica를 아니?)
Jack: No, I don't. (아니, 몰라.)

Jack: What does she look like?
(그녀는 어떻게 생겼니?)
Tom: She is tall and pretty. (그녀는 키가 크고 예뻐.)

Jack: What is she like? (그녀는 어떤 사람이니?)
Tom: She's very kind and outgoing.
(그녀는 매우 친절하고 외향적이야.)

Tom: Oh, here she comes! (오, 그녀가 여기 온다!)

P.12~13 DICTATION

A Listen and write the letters.

1 fat (뚱뚱한)
2 short (키가 작은)
3 thin (날씬한)
4 funny (재미있는)

B Listen and write the words.

1 Is she outgoing? (그녀는 외향적이니?)
2 Do you know Mrs. Brown?
(너 Brown 선생님을 아니?)
3 He's very lazy. (그는 매우 게을러.)
4 He is tall and has big blue eyes.
(그는 키가 크고 눈이 크고 파란색이야.)
5 What does your girlfriend look like?
(네 여자친구는 어떻게 생겼니?)

C Listen and fill in the blanks.

1 **G**: Do you know Kate? She's a new student.
(너 Kate를 아니? 그녀는 새로운 학생이야.)
B: No. What does she look like?
(아니. 그녀는 어떻게 생겼니?)
G: She is thin and has long hair.
(그녀는 날씬하고 머리가 길어.)

4

2 G: Who's that boy? (저 소년은 누구니?)
　　B: He's my new classmate, Ted.
　　　(그는 내 새로운 반 친구인 Ted야.)
　　G: He's tall and handsome!
　　　(그는 키가 크고 잘생겼구나!)
　　B: Yes, he is. (응, 맞아.)
　　G: What is he like? (그는 어떤 사람이니?)
　　B: He is a little shy. (그는 약간 수줍음이 많아.)

3 G: Do you know Tony? (너 Tony를 아니?)
　　B: No, I don't. Who is he?
　　　(아니, 몰라. 그는 누구니?)
　　G: He is Peter's brother. He's outgoing and
　　　funny.
　　　(그는 Peter의 남동생이야. 그는 외향적이고 재미있
　　　어.)
　　B: What does he look like? (그는 어떻게 생겼니?)
　　G: He is handsome and has big blue eyes.
　　　(그는 잘생겼고 눈이 크고 파란색이야.)
　　B: Is he tall? (그는 키가 크니?)
　　G: No, he's short and thin.
　　　(아니, 그는 키가 작고 날씬해.)

1 ⓐ shy (수줍음을 많이 타는)　ⓑ funny (재미있는)
　　ⓒ lazy (게으른)　　　　　ⓓ outgoing (외향적인)

2 ⓐ He is short and thin. (그는 키가 작고 날씬하다.)
　　ⓑ He is tall and fat. (그는 키가 크고 뚱뚱하다.)
　　ⓒ She is short and fat. (그녀는 키가 작고 뚱뚱하다.)
　　ⓓ She is tall and thin. (그녀는 키가 크고 날씬하다.)

3 G: Who is she? (그녀는 누구니?)
　　B: She's my cousin. (그녀는 내 사촌이야.)
　　G: What is she like? (그녀는 어떤 사람이니?)
　　B: She's kind and a little shy.
　　　(그녀는 친절하고 약간 수줍음이 많아.)

4 G: Do you know Joe? (너 Joe를 아니?)
　　B: No, I don't. What does he look like?
　　　(아니, 몰라. 그는 어떻게 생겼니?)
　　G: _____
　　ⓐ He is my classmate. (그는 내 반 친구야.)
　　ⓑ He is lazy. (그는 게을러.)
　　ⓒ He is very funny. (그는 매우 재미있어.)
　　ⓓ He is tall and handsome. (그는 키가 크고 잘생겼어.)

5 G: Who's that girl over there? (저기 저 소녀는 누구니?)
　　B: She's a new student. (그녀는 새로운 학생이야.)
　　G: Is she outgoing? (그녀는 외향적이니?)
　　B: _____

ⓐ Yes, she is my friend. (응, 그녀는 내 친구야.)
ⓑ No, she is not fat. (아니, 그녀는 뚱뚱하지 않아.)
ⓒ No, she's shy. (아니, 그녀는 수줍음이 많아.)
ⓓ Yes, she has long hair. (응, 그녀는 머리가 길어.)

6 ⓐ G: What is she like? (그녀는 어떤 사람이니?)
　　　B: She's very lazy. (그녀는 매우 게을러.)
　　ⓑ G: Is he tall? (그는 키가 크니?)
　　　B: No, he isn't. He's short.
　　　　(아니, 크지 않아. 그는 키가 작아.)
　　ⓒ G: Do you know Kate? (너 Kate를 아니?)
　　　B: No, I don't. Who is she?
　　　　(아니, 몰라. 그녀는 누구니?)
　　ⓓ G: What does your brother look like?
　　　　(네 형은 어떻게 생겼니?)
　　　B: He's outgoing and funny.
　　　　(그는 외향적이고 재미있어.)

7 B: Do you have a boyfriend? (너는 남자친구가 있니?)
　　G: Yes, I do. (응, 있어.)
　　B: What does he look like? (그는 어떻게 생겼니?)
　　G: He is handsome and has brown hair.
　　　(그는 잘생겼고 머리가 갈색이야.)
　　B: Is he tall? (그는 키가 크니?)
　　G: Yes, and he is thin. (응, 그리고 날씬해.)

Question: Who is the girl's boyfriend?
　　　　　(소녀의 남자친구는 누구인가?)

8 B: Do you know Lily? (너 Lily를 아니?)
　　G: No, I don't. Who is she? (아니, 몰라. 그녀는 누구니?)
　　B: She's a new student. She's very kind.
　　　(그녀는 새로운 학생이야. 그녀는 매우 친절해.)
　　G: What does she look like? (그녀는 어떻게 생겼니?)
　　B: She's short and has long hair.
　　　(그녀는 키가 작고 머리가 길어.)
　　G: Is she shy? (그녀는 수줍음을 많이 타니?)
　　B: No, she is outgoing. (아니, 그녀는 외향적이야.)

Question: What is Lily like? (Lily는 어떤 사람인가?)

UNIT 2 JOBS

ANSWERS

P.16

P.17

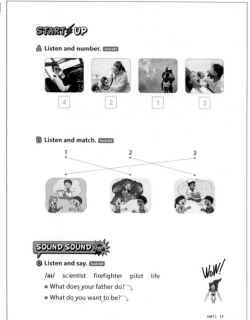

P.18

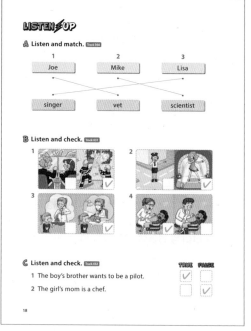

P.19

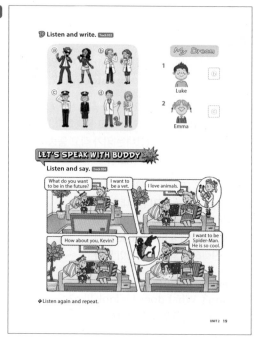

P.20~21 DICTATION

A 1 i   2 c, h   3 s, c, i   4 i, c, e

B 1 want   2 dentist   3 do
  4 vet   5 singer

C 1 scientist, science
  2 want, teacher, chef
  3 pilot, police, officer, firefighter

P.22~23 **UNIT TEST**

  1 ⓓ 2 ⓒ 3 ⓑ 4 ⓐ
  5 ⓒ 6 ⓓ 7 ⓒ 8 ⓑ

SCRIPTS & 해석

P.16 **ARE YOU READY?**

⚡ **Listen and number.**

  1 G: What does your father do?
    (너희 아빠는 무슨 일을 하시니?)
    B: He is a police officer. (경찰관이셔.)
    G: How cool! (멋지다!)

  2 G: What do you want to be?
    (너는 뭐가 되고 싶니?)
    B: I want to be a chef. I like to cook.
    (나는 요리사가 되고 싶어. 나는 요리하는 것을 좋아해.)

⭐ **Listen and repeat.**

  scientist (과학자)   singer (가수)
  police officer (경찰관)   firefighter (소방관)
  dentist (치과의사)   pilot (조종사)
  chef (요리사)   vet (수의사)

P.17 **START UP**

Ⓐ **Listen and number.**

  1 firefighter (소방관)
  2 vet (수의사)
  3 dentist (치과의사)
  4 pilot (조종사)

Ⓑ **Listen and match.**

  1 B: What do you want to be?
    (너는 뭐가 되고 싶니?)
    G: I want to be a singer. (나는 가수가 되고 싶어.)

  2 G: What does your father do?
    (너희 아빠는 무슨 일을 하시니?)
    B: He is a chef. (요리사이셔.)

  3 G: What do you want to be?
    (너는 뭐가 되고 싶니?)
    B: I want to be a scientist.
    (나는 과학자가 되고 싶어.)

P.17 **SOUND SOUND**

⬡ **Listen and say.**

  /ai/ scientist (과학자)   firefighter (소방관)
      pilot (조종사)   life (생명, 삶)
  ● What does your father do?
    (너희 아빠는 무슨 일을 하시니?)
  ● What do you want to be? (너는 뭐가 되고 싶니?)

P.18~19 **LISTEN UP**

Ⓐ **Listen and match.**

  1 G: Joe, what do you want to be?
    (Joe, 너는 뭐가 되고 싶니?)
    B: I want to be a vet. I like animals.
    (나는 수의사가 되고 싶어. 나는 동물을 좋아해.)

  2 G: Mike, what do you want to be?
    (Mike, 너는 뭐가 되고 싶니?)
    B: I want to be a scientist. My favorite subject
    is science.
    (나는 과학자가 되고 싶어. 내가 가장 좋아하는 과목
    은 과학이야.)

  3 B: Lisa, what do you want to be?
    (Lisa, 너는 뭐가 되고 싶니?)
    G: I want to be a singer. I like to sing and dance.
    (나는 가수가 되고 싶어. 나는 노래하고 춤추는 것을
    좋아해.)

Ⓑ **Listen and check.**

  1 G: What does your mother do?
    (너희 엄마는 무슨 일을 하시니?)
    B: She is a firefighter. (소방관이셔.)
    G: How about your father? (너희 아빠는?)
    B: He is a firefighter, too. I'm proud of them.
    (아빠도 소방관이셔. 나는 그들이 자랑스러워.)

  2 G: What do you want to be? (너는 뭐가 되고 싶니?)
    B: I want to be a police officer.
    (나는 경찰관이 되고 싶어.)
    G: What does your twin sister want to be?
    (네 쌍둥이 여동생은 뭐가 되고 싶어 하니?)
    B: She wants to be a singer. She sings very well.
    (그녀는 가수가 되고 싶어 해. 그녀는 노래를 아주 잘해.)

  3 B: What does your father do?
    (너희 아빠는 무슨 일을 하시니?)
    G: He's a scientist. (과학자이셔.)
    B: What do you want to be in the future? Do
    you want to be a scientist, too?
    (너는 미래에 뭐가 되고 싶니? 너도 과학자가 되고 싶니?)

G: No, I want to be a vet.
(아니, 나는 수의사가 되고 싶어.)

4 B: What do you want to be in the future?
(너는 미래에 뭐가 되고 싶니?)
G: I want to be a dentist.
(나는 치과의사가 되고 싶어.)
B: Your mom and dad are dentists, right?
(너희 엄마랑 아빠는 치과의사이시지, 그렇지?)
G: My mom is a dentist. But my dad is a chef.
(엄마는 치과의사이셔. 하지만 아빠는 요리사이셔.)

C Listen and check.

1 G: What does your father do?
(너희 아빠는 무슨 일을 하시니?)
B: He's a pilot. (조종사이셔.)
G: Do you want to be a pilot, too?
(너도 조종사가 되고 싶니?)
B: No, I want to be a doctor.
(아니, 나는 의사가 되고 싶어.)
G: How about your brother? What does he want to be?
(너희 형은 어때? 그는 뭐가 되고 싶어 하니?)
B: He wants to be a pilot like my father.
(그는 아빠처럼 조종사가 되고 싶어 해.)

Question: The boy's brother wants to be a pilot.
(소년의 형은 조종사가 되고 싶어 한다.)

2 G: What do you want to be, Nick?
(Nick, 너는 뭐가 되고 싶니?)
B: I want to be an English teacher. I like English. How about you?
(나는 영어 선생님이 되고 싶어. 나는 영어를 좋아해. 너는 어때?)
G: I want to be a chef. I like to cook.
(나는 요리사가 되고 싶어. 나는 요리하는 것을 좋아해.)
B: Oh, really? My mom is a chef.
(오, 정말? 우리 엄마가 요리사이셔.)
G: How wonderful! (멋지다!)

Question: The girl's mom is a chef.
(소녀의 엄마는 요리사이다.)

D Listen and write.

1 B: What do you want to be in the future?
(너는 미래에 뭐가 되고 싶니?)
G: I want to be a singer. I like to sing and dance. What about you, Luke?
(나는 가수가 되고 싶어. 나는 노래하고 춤추는 것을 좋아해. 너는 어때, Luke?)

B: I want to be a scientist. My dad is a scientist. I want to be like him.
(나는 과학자가 되고 싶어. 우리 아빠가 과학자이셔. 나는 아빠처럼 되고 싶어.)
G: Wow, that's great! (와, 그거 멋지다!)

2 B: Emma, is your father a vet?
(Emma, 너희 아빠는 수의사이시니?)
G: Yes, he is. He helps sick animals.
(응, 맞아. 아빠는 아픈 동물들을 도와주셔.)
B: What do you want to be in the future?
(너는 미래에 뭐가 되고 싶니?)
G: I want to be a police officer. I like to help people.
(나는 경찰관이 되고 싶어. 나는 사람들을 돕는 것을 좋아해.)
B: Oh, really? I'm glad to hear that.
(오, 정말? 그 말을 들으니 기뻐.)

P.19 LET'S SPEAK WITH BUDDY

Listen and say.

Kevin: What do you want to be in the future?
(누나는 미래에 뭐가 되고 싶어?)
Ann: I want to be a vet. (나는 수의사가 되고 싶어.)

Ann: I love animals. (나는 동물을 좋아해.)

Ann: How about you, Kevin? (너는 어때, Kevin?)

Kevin: I want to be Spider-Man. He is so cool.
(나는 스파이더맨이 되고 싶어. 그는 정말 멋져.)

P.20~21 DICTATION

A Listen and write the letters.

1 pilot (조종사)
2 chef (요리사)
3 scientist (과학자)
4 police officer (경찰관)

B Listen and write the words.

1 What do you want to be? (너는 뭐가 되고 싶니?)
2 I want to be a dentist. (나는 치과의사가 되고 싶어.)
3 What does your mother do?
(너희 엄마는 무슨 일을 하시니?)
4 Is your father a vet? (너희 아빠는 수의사이시니?)
5 Do you want to be a singer, too?
(너도 가수가 되고 싶니?)

C Listen and fill in the blanks.

1 G: Mike, what do you want to be?

(Mike, 너는 뭐가 되고 싶니?)

B: I want to be a scientist. My favorite subject is science.
(나는 과학자가 되고 싶어. 내가 가장 좋아하는 과목은 과학이야.)

2 G: What do you want to be, Nick?
(Nick, 너는 뭐가 되고 싶니?)

B: I want to be an English teacher. I like English. How about you?
(나는 영어 선생님이 되고 싶어. 나는 영어를 좋아해. 너는 어때?)

G: I want to be a chef. I like to cook.
(나는 요리사가 되고 싶어. 나는 요리하는 것을 좋아해.)

B: Oh, really? My mom is a chef.
(오, 정말? 우리 엄마가 요리사이셔.)

G: How wonderful! (멋지다!)

3 G: What does your father do?
(너희 아빠는 무슨 일을 하시니?)

B: He's a pilot. (조종사이셔.)

G: Do you want to be a pilot, too?
(너도 조종사가 되고 싶니?)

B: No, I want to be a police officer.
(아니, 나는 경찰관이 되고 싶어.)

G: How about your brother? What does he want to be?
(너희 형은 어때? 그는 뭐가 되고 싶어 하니?)

B: He wants to be a firefighter.
(그는 소방관이 되고 싶어 해.)

P.22-23 UNIT TEST

1 ⓐ dentist (치과의사) ⓑ police officer (경찰관)
ⓒ singer (가수) ⓓ firefighter (소방관)

2 ⓐ The boy wants to be a pilot.
(소년은 조종사가 되고 싶어 한다.)
ⓑ The girl wants to be a chef.
(소녀는 요리사가 되고 싶어 한다.)
ⓒ The boy wants to be a scientist.
(소년은 과학자가 되고 싶어 한다.)
ⓓ The girl wants to be a vet.
(소녀는 수의사가 되고 싶어 한다.)

3 B: What do you want to be? (너는 뭐가 되고 싶니?)
G: I want to be a singer. (나는 가수가 되고 싶어.)
B: Do you sing well? (너 노래 잘하니?)
G: Yes, I do. (응, 잘해.)

4 G: What does your father do?

(너희 아빠는 무슨 일을 하시니?)

B: He is a dentist. (치과의사이셔.)

G: Do you want to be a dentist, too?
(너도 치과의사가 되고 싶니?)

B: _____

ⓐ No, I don't. (아니, 그렇지 않아.)

ⓑ Yes, my brother wants to be a dentist.
(응, 내 남동생은 치과의사가 되고 싶어 해.)

ⓒ I'm glad to hear that. (그 말을 들으니 기뻐.)

ⓓ No, I want to be a dentist.
(아니, 나는 치과의사가 되고 싶어.)

5 B: What do you want to be? (너는 뭐가 되고 싶니?)

G: I want to be a firefighter.
(나는 소방관이 되고 싶어.)

B: What does your brother want to be?
(네 남동생은 뭐가 되고 싶어 하니?)

G: _____

ⓐ He is a firefighter. (그는 소방관이야.)

ⓑ I want to be a scientist. (나는 과학자가 되고 싶어.)

ⓒ He wants to be a firefighter, too.
(그도 소방관이 되고 싶어 해.)

ⓓ My father is a police officer.
(우리 아빠는 경찰관이셔.)

6 ⓐ G: I want to be a chef. (나는 요리사가 되고 싶어.)
B: Oh, really? I want to be a chef, too.
(오, 정말? 나도 요리사가 되고 싶어.)

ⓑ G: What does your sister want to be?
(네 여동생은 뭐가 되고 싶어 하니?)
B: She wants to be a pilot.
(그녀는 조종사가 되고 싶어 해.)

ⓒ G: What does your mother do?
(너희 엄마는 무슨 일을 하시니?)
B: She is a vet. (수의사이셔.)

ⓓ G: Does he want to be a scientist?
(그는 과학자가 되고 싶어 하니?)
B: No, I'm a doctor. (아니, 나는 의사야.)

7 G: What do you want to be? (너는 뭐가 되고 싶니?)
B: I want to be a pilot. How about you?
(나는 조종사가 되고 싶어. 너는 어때?)
G: I want to be a police officer. I like to help people.
(나는 경찰관이 되고 싶어. 나는 사람들을 돕는 것을 좋아해.)
B: Oh, really? My dad is a police officer.
(오, 정말? 우리 아빠가 경찰관이셔.)
G: How cool! (멋지다!)

Question: What does the boy's father do?
(소년의 아빠는 무슨 일을 하는가?)

8 **G**: What do you want to be in the future?
(너는 미래에 뭐가 되고 싶니?)

B: I want to be a chef. I like to cook. What about you?
(나는 요리사가 되고 싶어. 나는 요리하는 것을 좋아해. 너는 어때?)

G: I want to be a vet. My mom is a vet. I want to be like her.
(나는 수의사가 되고 싶어. 우리 엄마가 수의사이셔. 나는 엄마처럼 되고 싶어.)

B: Wow, that's great! (와, 그거 멋지다!)

Question: What does the girl want to be?
(소녀는 무엇이 되고 싶어 하는가?)

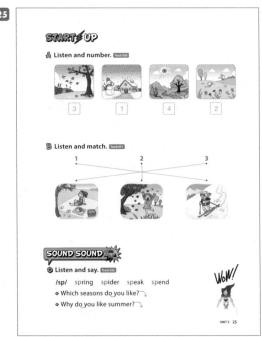

P.26

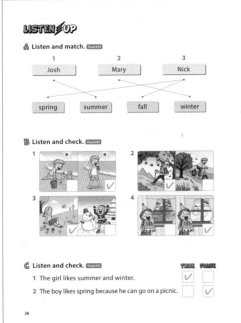

LISTEN UP

A Listen and match. `Track 053`

1	2	3
Josh	Mary	Nick

spring summer fall winter

B Listen and check. `Track 054`

1 ... ✓
2 ... ✓
3 ... ✓
4 ... ✓

C Listen and check. `Track 055`

	TRUE	FALSE
1 The girl likes summer and winter.	✓	
2 The boy likes spring because he can go on a picnic.		✓

26

P.27

D Listen and write. `Track 056`

ⓐ ⓑ ⓒ ⓓ

1 Ted ⓐ
2 Joe ⓒ

LET'S SPEAK WITH BUDDY

Listen and say. `Track 057`

I don't like summer. It's too hot.
Which seasons do you like?
I like winter. I like to go skiing.
How about you?
I like summer.
Because I like to play at the beach.
Why do you like it?

❖Listen again and repeat.

UNIT 3 27

P.28~29 DICTATION

A 1 picnic 2 leaves 3 beach 4 skiing

B 1 seasons 2 spring 3 Why
4 colorful 5 winter

C 1 summer, Because
2 Which, seasons, winter, go, skiing, swimming
3 fall, spring, go, on, play

P.30~31 UNIT TEST

1 ⓐ 2 ⓒ 3 ⓑ 4 ⓒ
5 ⓑ 6 ⓓ 7 ⓒ 8 ⓓ

SCRIPTS & 해석

P.24 ARE YOU READY?

⚡ **Listen and number.**

1 G: Which seasons do you like?
   (너는 어느 계절을 좋아하니?)
   B: I like fall because I can see colorful leaves.
   (나는 형형색색의 나뭇잎을 볼 수 있기 때문에 가을을 좋아해.)

2 G: Why do you like summer?
   (너는 왜 여름을 좋아하니?)
   B: Because I can play at the beach.
   (왜냐하면 해변에서 놀 수 있기 때문이야.)

⭐ **Listen and repeat.**

spring (봄)   summer (여름)
fall (가을)   winter (겨울)

go on a picnic (소풍을 가다)
play at the beach (해변에서 놀다)
see colorful leaves (형형색색의 나뭇잎을 보다)
go skiing (스키 타러 가다)

P.25 START UP

A Listen and number.

1 winter (겨울)
2 spring (봄)
3 fall (가을)
4 summer (여름)

B Listen and match.

1 G: Which seasons do you like?
   (너는 어느 계절을 좋아하니?)
   B: I like winter. I like to go skiing.
   (나는 겨울을 좋아해. 나는 스키 타러 가는 것을 좋아해.)

2 B: Why do you like fall? (너는 왜 가을을 좋아하니?)
   G: Because I can see colorful leaves.

(왜냐하면 형형색색의 나뭇잎을 볼 수 있기 때문이야.)

3 B: Why do you like spring?
   (너는 왜 봄을 좋아하니?)
G: Because I like to go on a picnic.
   (왜냐하면 소풍 가는 것을 좋아하기 때문이야.)

P.25 SOUND SOUND

🎧 Listen and say.

/sp/ spring (봄)   spider (거미)
     speak (말하다)   spend (쓰다, 소비하다)
   ○ Which seasons do you like?
     (너는 어느 계절을 좋아하니?)
   ○ Why do you like summer?
     (너는 왜 여름을 좋아하니?)

P.26~27 LISTEN UP

Ⓐ Listen and match.

1 G: Josh, which seasons do you like?
   (Josh, 너는 어느 계절을 좋아하니?)
B: I like summer because I can play at the beach.
   (나는 해변에서 놀 수 있기 때문에 여름을 좋아해.)

2 B: Mary, which seasons do you like?
   (Mary, 너는 어느 계절을 좋아하니?)
G: I like winter because I like to go skiing.
   (나는 스키 타러 가는 것을 좋아하기 때문에 겨울을 좋아해.)

3 G: Nick, which seasons do you like?
   (Nick, 너는 어느 계절을 좋아하니?)
B: I like spring and fall because the weather is nice. (나는 날씨가 좋기 때문에 봄과 가을을 좋아해.)

Ⓑ Listen and check.

1 G: Which seasons do you like?
   (너는 어느 계절을 좋아하니?)
B: I like summer. (나는 여름을 좋아해.)
G: Why do you like it? (너는 왜 여름을 좋아하니?)
B: Because I can eat lots of ice cream.
   (왜냐하면 아이스크림을 많이 먹을 수 있기 때문이야.)

2 B: Do you like fall? (너는 가을을 좋아하니?)
G: Yes, because I can see colorful leaves in fall.
   How about you?
   (응, 왜냐하면 가을에는 형형색색의 나뭇잎을 볼 수 있기 때문이야. 너는 어때?)
B: I like fall, too. (나도 가을을 좋아해.)
G: Why do you like it? (너는 왜 가을을 좋아하니?)

B: Because I like to go hiking.
   (왜냐하면 등산하러 가는 것을 좋아하기 때문이야.)

3 G: Which seasons do you like?
   (너는 어느 계절을 좋아하니?)
B: I like winter. Do you like winter, too?
   (나는 겨울을 좋아해. 너도 겨울을 좋아하니?)
G: No, I don't. It's too cold.
   (아니, 좋아하지 않아. 너무 추워.)
B: Which seasons do you like, then?
   (그럼, 너는 어느 계절을 좋아하니?)
G: I like spring. It's warm.
   (나는 봄을 좋아해. 따뜻하잖아.)

4 B: I like fall. Which seasons do you like, Lisa?
   (나는 가을을 좋아해. Lisa, 너는 어느 계절을 좋아하니?)
G: I like winter. (나는 겨울을 좋아해.)
B: Why do you like it? (너는 왜 겨울을 좋아하니?)
G: Because my birthday is in winter.
   (왜냐하면 내 생일이 겨울에 있기 때문이야.)

Ⓒ Listen and check.

1 B: Do you like fall? (너는 가을을 좋아하니?)
G: No, I don't. (아니, 좋아하지 않아.)
B: Then, which seasons do you like?
   (그럼, 너는 어느 계절을 좋아하니?)
G: I like summer and winter.
   (나는 여름과 겨울을 좋아해.)
B: Why do you like summer and winter?
   (너는 왜 여름과 겨울을 좋아하니?)
G: Because I can play at the beach in summer, and I can make a snowman in winter.
   (왜냐하면 여름에는 해변에서 놀 수 있고, 겨울에는 눈사람을 만들 수 있기 때문이야.)

Question: The girl likes summer and winter.
   (소녀는 여름과 겨울을 좋아한다.)

2 B: Do you like spring? (너는 봄을 좋아하니?)
G: Yes, I do. I like to go on a picnic in spring.
   How about you?
   (응, 좋아해. 나는 봄에 소풍 가는 것을 좋아해. 너는 어때?)
B: I like spring, too. (나도 봄을 좋아해.)
G: Why do you like it? (너는 왜 봄을 좋아하니?)
B: Because I like the warm weather in spring.
   (왜냐하면 봄의 따뜻한 날씨를 좋아하기 때문이야.)

Question: The boy likes spring because he can go on a picnic.
   (소년은 소풍을 갈 수 있기 때문에 봄을 좋아한다.)

D Listen and write.

1 B: Which seasons do you like?
(너는 어느 계절을 좋아하니?)
G: I like winter. (나는 겨울을 좋아해.)
B: Why do you like it? (너는 왜 겨울을 좋아하니?)
G: Because I like to go skiing. Do you like winter, too, Ted?
(왜냐하면 스키 타러 가는 것을 좋아하기 때문이야. Ted, 너도 겨울을 좋아하니?)
B: No, I don't. I like summer. I like to go swimming.
(아니, 좋아하지 않아. 나는 여름을 좋아해. 나는 수영하러 가는 것을 좋아해.)

2 G: Joe, do you like fall?
(Joe, 너는 가을을 좋아하니?)
B: Yes, I do. How about you?
(응, 좋아해. 너는 어때?)
G: I like it, too. I like to go hiking in fall. Why do you like fall?
(나도 가을을 좋아해. 나는 가을에 등산하러 가는 것을 좋아해. 너는 왜 가을을 좋아하니?)
B: Because I can see colorful leaves.
(왜냐하면 형형색색의 나뭇잎을 볼 수 있기 때문이야.)

P.27 LET'S SPEAK WITH BUDDY

Listen and say.

Tom: I don't like summer. It's too hot.
(나는 여름을 좋아하지 않아. 너무 더워.)
Jack: Which seasons do you like?
(너는 어느 계절을 좋아하니?)
Tom: I like winter. I like to go skiing. How about you?
(나는 겨울을 좋아해. 나는 스키 타러 가는 것을 좋아해. 너는 어때?)
Jack: I like summer. (나는 여름을 좋아해.)
Tom: Why do you like it? (너는 왜 여름을 좋아하니?)
Jack: Because I like to play at the beach.
(왜냐하면 해변에서 노는 것을 좋아하기 때문이야.)

P.28~29 DICTATION

A Listen and write the words.

1 go on a picnic (소풍을 가다)
2 see colorful leaves (형형색색의 나뭇잎을 보다)
3 play at the beach (해변에서 놀다)
4 go skiing (스키 타러 가다)

B Listen and write the words.

1 Which seasons do you like?
(너는 어느 계절을 좋아하니?)
2 I like spring. (나는 봄을 좋아해.)
3 Why do you like fall? (너는 왜 가을을 좋아하니?)
4 Because I can see colorful leaves.
(왜냐하면 형형색색의 나뭇잎을 볼 수 있기 때문이야.)
5 Do you like winter? (너는 겨울을 좋아하니?)

C Listen and fill in the blanks.

1 G: Which seasons do you like?
(너는 어느 계절을 좋아하니?)
B: I like summer. (나는 여름을 좋아해.)
G: Why do you like it? (너는 왜 여름을 좋아하니?)
B: Because I can eat lots of ice cream.
(왜냐하면 아이스크림을 많이 먹을 수 있기 때문이야.)

2 B: Which seasons do you like?
(너는 어느 계절을 좋아하니?)
G: I like winter. (나는 겨울을 좋아해.)
B: Why do you like it? (너는 왜 겨울을 좋아하니?)
G: Because I like to go skiing. Do you like winter, too, Ted?
(왜냐하면 스키 타러 가는 것을 좋아하기 때문이야. Ted, 너도 겨울을 좋아하니?)
B: No, I don't. I like summer. I like to go swimming.
(아니, 좋아하지 않아. 나는 여름을 좋아해. 나는 수영하러 가는 것을 좋아해.)

3 B: Do you like fall? (너는 가을을 좋아하니?)
G: No, I don't. (아니, 좋아하지 않아.)
B: Then, which seasons do you like?
(그럼, 너는 어느 계절을 좋아하니?)
G: I like spring and summer.
(나는 봄과 여름을 좋아해.)
B: Why do you like spring and summer?
(너는 왜 봄과 여름을 좋아하니?)
G: Because I can go on a picnic in spring, and I can play at the beach in summer.
(왜냐하면 봄에는 소풍을 갈 수 있고, 여름에는 해변에서 놀 수 있기 때문이야.)

P.30~31 UNIT TEST

1 ⓐ spring (봄)   ⓑ summer (여름)
ⓒ fall (가을)   ⓓ winter (겨울)

2 ⓐ He likes to go on a picnic.
(그는 소풍 가는 것을 좋아한다.)
ⓑ He likes to play at the beach.
(그는 해변에서 노는 것을 좋아한다.)

ⓒ He likes to see colorful leaves.
(그는 형형색색의 나뭇잎을 보는 것을 좋아한다.)

ⓓ He likes to go skiing.
(그는 스키 타러 가는 것을 좋아한다.)

3 B: Do you like winter? (너는 겨울을 좋아하니?)
   G: No, I don't. It's too cold.
      (아니, 좋아하지 않아. 너무 추워.)
   B: Which seasons do you like, then?
      (그럼, 너는 어느 계절을 좋아하니?)
   G: I like spring because I like warm days.
      (나는 따뜻한 날을 좋아하기 때문에 봄을 좋아해.)

4 ⓐ B: Which seasons do you like?
         (너는 어느 계절을 좋아하니?)
      G: I like winter because my birthday is in
         winter.
         (나는 내 생일이 겨울에 있기 때문에 겨울을 좋아해.)
   ⓑ G: Which seasons do you like?
         (너는 어느 계절을 좋아하니?)
      B: I like summer because I can eat lots of ice
         cream.
         (나는 아이스크림을 많이 먹을 수 있기 때문에 여름을
         좋아해.)
   ⓒ B: Which seasons do you like?
         (너는 어느 계절을 좋아하니?)
      G: I like summer because I can play at the
         beach.
         (나는 해변에서 놀 수 있기 때문에 여름을 좋아해.)
   ⓓ G: Which seasons do you like?
         (너는 어느 계절을 좋아하니?)
      B: I like winter because I can make a snowman.
         (나는 눈사람을 만들 수 있기 때문에 겨울을 좋아해.)

5 G: Do you like fall? (너는 가을을 좋아하니?)
   B: Yes, because I can see colorful leaves. How
      about you?
      (응, 왜냐하면 형형색색의 나뭇잎을 볼 수 있기 때문이야.
      너는 어때?)
   G: _____
   ⓐ Which seasons do you like?
      (너는 어느 계절을 좋아하니?)
   ⓑ I like fall, too. (나도 가을을 좋아해.)
   ⓒ Why do you like fall? (너는 왜 가을을 좋아하니?)
   ⓓ Because I like to go hiking.
      (왜냐하면 등산하러 가는 것을 좋아하기 때문이야.)

6 ⓐ G: Which seasons do you like?
         (너는 어느 계절을 좋아하니?)
      B: I like spring. (나는 봄을 좋아해.)
   ⓑ G: Do you like fall? (너는 가을을 좋아하니?)
      B: No, I don't like fall.

(아니, 나는 가을을 좋아하지 않아.)
   ⓒ G: I don't like winter. How about you?
         (나는 겨울을 좋아하지 않아. 너는 어때?)
      B: I like it because I like to go skiing.
         (나는 스키 타러 가는 것을 좋아하기 때문에 겨울을
         좋아해.)
   ⓓ G: Why do you like summer?
         (너는 왜 여름을 좋아하니?)
      B: Yes, I like fall. (응, 나는 가을을 좋아해.)

7 B: Do you like spring? (너는 봄을 좋아하니?)
   G: Yes, I do. My birthday is in spring. How about
      you? (응, 좋아해. 내 생일이 봄에 있어. 너는 어때?)
   B: I like winter. (나는 겨울을 좋아해.)
   G: Why do you like it? (너는 왜 겨울을 좋아하니?)
   B: Because I like to go skiing.
      (왜냐하면 스키 타러 가는 것을 좋아하기 때문이야.)

   Question: Which season does the boy like?
             (소년은 어느 계절을 좋아하는가?)

8 B: Which seasons do you like?
      (너는 어느 계절을 좋아하니?)
   G: I like summer. (나는 여름을 좋아해.)
   B: Why do you like it? (너는 왜 여름을 좋아하니?)
   G: Because I like to play at the beach. Do you like
      summer, too?
      (왜냐하면 해변에서 노는 것을 좋아하기 때문이야. 너도
      여름을 좋아하니?)
   B: No, it's too hot. I like fall. I like cool days.
      (아니, 너무 더워. 나는 가을을 좋아해. 나는 시원한 날을
      좋아해.)

   Question: Why does the girl like summer?
             (소녀는 왜 여름을 좋아하는가?)
   ⓐ Because she likes to go hiking.
      (왜냐하면 그녀는 등산하러 가는 것을 좋아하기 때문이다.)
   ⓑ Because she likes to go swimming.
      (왜냐하면 그녀는 수영하러 가는 것을 좋아하기 때문이다.)
   ⓒ Because she likes to eat ice cream.
      (왜냐하면 그녀는 아이스크림을 먹는 것을 좋아하기 때문
      이다.)
   ⓓ Because she likes to play at the beach.
      (왜냐하면 그녀는 해변에서 노는 것을 좋아하기 때문이다.)

P.32~33

REVIEW TEST 1 UNITS 1~3

| 1 ⓑ | 2 ⓓ | 3 ⓒ | 4 ⓓ | 5 ⓐ |
| 6 ⓒ | 7 ⓓ | 8 ⓒ | 9 ⓐ | 10 ⓓ |

1 ⓐ shy (수줍음을 많이 타는)   ⓑ funny (재미있는)

ⓒ lazy (게으른)   ⓓ outgoing (외향적인)

2 ⓐ singer (가수)   ⓑ pilot (조종사)
   ⓒ scientist (과학자)   ⓓ dentist (치과의사)

3 G: Do you like summer? (너는 여름을 좋아하니?)
   B: No, it's too hot. How about you?
      (아니, 너무 더워. 너는 어때?)
   G: I like summer because I can play at the beach.
      (나는 해변에서 놀 수 있기 때문에 여름을 좋아해.)

4 G: Who is he? (그는 누구니?)
   B: He's my cousin. (그는 내 사촌이야.)
   G: He looks nice. What is he like?
      (멋져 보인다. 그는 어떤 사람이니?)
   B: _____
   ⓐ He is tall and thin. (그는 키가 크고 날씬해.)
   ⓑ He is my uncle. (그는 우리 삼촌이야.)
   ⓒ He has blue eyes. (그는 눈이 파란색이야.)
   ⓓ He is a little shy. (그는 약간 수줍음이 많아.)

5 B: What does your father do?
      (너희 아빠는 무슨 일을 하시니?)
   G: He is a vet. He helps sick animals.
      (수의사셔. 아빠는 아픈 동물들을 도와주셔.)
   B: How about your mother? (너희 엄마는?)
   G: _____
   ⓐ She is a pilot. (엄마는 조종사이셔.)
   ⓑ She wants to be a vet.
      (엄마는 수의사가 되고 싶어 하셔.)
   ⓒ She likes animals. (엄마는 동물을 좋아하셔.)
   ⓓ She is a firefighter, too. (엄마도 소방관이셔.)

6 ⓐ B: Is your brother lazy? (네 남동생은 게으르니?)
      G: Yes, he is. (응, 게을러.)
   ⓑ B: Why do you like fall? (너는 왜 가을을 좋아하니?)
      G: Because I can see colorful leaves.
         (왜냐하면 형형색색의 나뭇잎을 볼 수 있기 때문이야.)
   ⓒ B: Do you know Peter? (너 Peter를 아니?)
      G: No, but he is tall. (아니, 하지만 그는 키가 커.)
   ⓓ B: What does your sister want to be?
         (네 여동생은 뭐가 되고 싶어 하니?)
      G: She wants to be a singer.
         (그녀는 가수가 되고 싶어 해.)

7 ⓐ G: Which seasons do you like?
         (너는 어느 계절을 좋아하니?)
      B: I like spring and fall. (나는 봄과 가을을 좋아해.)
   ⓑ G: What does she look like?
         (그녀는 어떻게 생겼니?)
      B: She is short and has brown hair.
         (그녀는 키가 작고 머리가 갈색이야.)
   ⓒ G: Is your mother a dentist?

      (너희 엄마는 치과의사이시니?)
      B: No, she is a teacher. (아니, 선생님이셔.)
   ⓓ G: Do you like summer, too?
         (너도 여름을 좋아하니?)
      B: Yes. My birthday is in winter.
         (응. 내 생일이 겨울에 있어.)

8 B: What do you want to be? (너는 뭐가 되고 싶니?)
   G: I want to be a chef. I like to cook. What about
      you?
      (나는 요리사가 되고 싶어. 나는 요리하는 것을 좋아해.
      너는 어때?)
   B: I want to be a scientist. (나는 과학자가 되고 싶어.)
   G: Your dad is a scientist, right?
      (너희 아빠가 과학자이시지, 그렇지?)
   B: Yes, he is. I want to be like him.
      (응, 맞아. 나는 아빠처럼 되고 싶어.)
   G: Wow. That's great! (와. 그거 멋지다!)

   Question: Who is the boy's dad?
            (누가 소년의 아빠인가?)

9 G: Which seasons do you like?
      (너는 어느 계절을 좋아하니?)
   B: I like winter. (나는 겨울을 좋아해.)
   G: Why do you like it? (너는 왜 겨울을 좋아하니?)
   B: Because I can go skiing. Do you like winter,
      too?
      (왜냐하면 스키 타러 갈 수 있기 때문이야. 너도 겨울을
      좋아하니?)
   G: No, it's too cold. I like spring because I like to
      go on a picnic.
      (아니, 너무 추워. 나는 소풍 가는 것을 좋아하기 때문에
      봄을 좋아해.)

   Question: Which season does the girl like?
            (소녀는 어느 계절을 좋아하는가?)

10 B: Do you know Lisa? (너 Lisa를 아니?)
   G: No, I don't. Who is she?
      (아니, 몰라. 그녀는 누구니?)
   B: She's a new student. She's kind and outgoing.
      (그녀는 새로운 학생이야. 그녀는 친절하고 외향적이야.)
   G: What does she look like? Is she tall?
      (그녀는 어떻게 생겼니? 키가 크니?)
   B: No, she is short and thin.
      (아니, 그녀는 키가 작고 날씬해.)

   Question: What does Lisa look like?
            (Lisa는 어떻게 생겼는가?)
   ⓐ She is tall and fat. (그녀는 키가 크고 뚱뚱하다.)
   ⓑ She is tall and thin. (그녀는 키가 크고 날씬하다.)
   ⓒ She is short and fat. (그녀는 키가 작고 뚱뚱하다.)
   ⓓ She is short and thin. (그녀는 키가 작고 날씬하다.)

UNIT 4 SICKNESS

ANSWERS

P.34

P.35

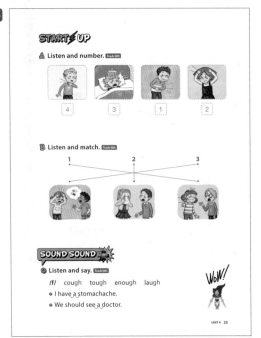

P.36

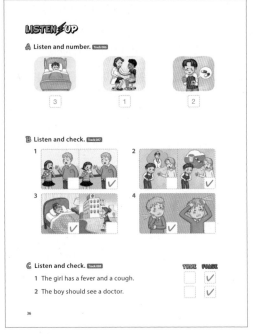

P.37

P.38~39 DICTATION

A 1 g, h   2 o, o   3 c, i   4 t, h

B 1 wrong   2 cold   3 doctor
       4 fever   5 headache

C 1 toothache, dentist
  2 stomachache, medicine
  3 cold, cough, headache
  4 sore, throat, runny, nose

UNIT TEST

  1 ⓑ   2 ⓓ   3 ⓒ   4 ⓐ
  5 ⓓ   6 ⓒ   7 ⓑ   8 ⓐ

SCRIPTS & 해석

ARE YOU READY?

⚡ **Listen and number.**

  1 W: Are you okay? What's wrong?
     (너 괜찮니? 어디 아프니?)
   G: I have a stomachache. (배가 아파요.)
   W: Oh, take this medicine. (오, 이 약을 먹으렴.)

  2 W: Do you have a fever? (너 열이 나니?)
   G: Yes, I do. (네.)
   W: We should see a doctor. (병원에 가야겠구나.)

⭐ **Listen and repeat.**

headache (두통)   toothache (치통)
stomachache (복통)   fever (열)
cough (기침)   runny nose (콧물)
sore throat (인후염(목 아픔))

see a doctor (병원에 가다)
take medicine (약을 먹다)

START UP

Ⓐ **Listen and number.**

  1 stomachache (복통)
  2 headache (두통)
  3 fever (열)
  4 sore throat (인후염(목 아픔))

Ⓑ **Listen and match.**

  1 B: Are you okay? What's wrong?
     (너 괜찮니? 어디 아프니?)
   G: I have a toothache. (이가 아파.)

  2 B: Do you have a runny nose? (너 콧물이 나니?)
   G: Yes. I have a cough, too. (응. 기침도 해.)

  3 G: I have a headache. (나 머리가 아파.)
   B: Oh, you should take some medicine.
     (오, 너 약을 좀 먹어야겠다.)

SOUND SOUND

🔊 **Listen and say.**

/f/ cough (기침)   tough (힘든, 어려운)
    enough (충분한)   laugh (웃다)
  ○ I have a stomachache. (나는 배가 아파.)
  ○ We should see a doctor. (병원에 가야겠다.)

LISTEN UP

Ⓐ **Listen and number.**

  1 G: Are you okay? What's wrong?
     (너 괜찮니? 어디 아프니?)
   B: I have a fever. (열이 나.)
   G: Oh, you should see a doctor.
     (오, 너 병원에 가야겠다.)

  2 G: Do you have a stomachache?
     (너 배가 아프니?)
   B: Yes, I do. (응.)
   G: Maybe you should take some medicine.
     (너 약을 좀 먹어야 할 것 같아.)

  3 G: Are you okay? What's wrong?
     (너 괜찮니? 어디 아프니?)
   B: I have a sore throat and a cough.
     (목이 아프고 기침을 해.)
   G: You should rest at home.
     (너 집에서 쉬어야겠다.)

Ⓑ **Listen and check.**

  1 M: Are you okay? You don't look good.
     (너 괜찮니? 안색이 안 좋아 보이는구나.)
   G: I have a fever. (저 열이 나요.)
   M: Do you have a sore throat, too?
     (목도 아프니?)
   G: No, but I have a runny nose.
     (아뇨, 하지만 콧물이 나요.)
   M: Let's go to the doctor. (병원에 가자.)

  2 W: Do you want some ice cream?
     (아이스크림 좀 먹겠니?)
   B: No thanks, Mom. I have a stomachache.
     (아뇨, 괜찮아요, 엄마. 저 배가 아파요.)
   W: Oh, then you shouldn't eat any more. You
     should take some medicine.
     (오, 그럼 더 이상 먹지 않는 게 좋겠다. 너 약을 좀 먹
     어야겠다.)
   B: Okay, I will. (네, 그럴게요.)

  3 G: Achoo! (에취!)
   B: Bless you! Do you have a cold?
     (저런, 몸조심해! 너 감기 걸렸니?)

17

G: Yes, I have a cough and a headache.
   (응, 기침이 나고 머리가 아파.)
B: Oh, you should rest at home.
   (오, 너 집에서 쉬어야겠다.)
G: Okay, I will. (응, 그럴게.)

4 B: Should I go to school? (저 학교에 가야 해요?)
   W: Why? What's wrong? (왜 그러니? 어디 아프니?)
   B: I have a toothache. (이가 아파요.)
   W: Let me check. (pause) Maybe we should
      see a dentist.
      (어디 보자. 치과에 가야 할 것 같구나.)
   G: Okay, Mom. (알겠어요, 엄마.)

C Listen and check.

1 B: Are you okay? You don't look good.
   (너 괜찮니? 안색이 안 좋아 보여.)
   G: I have a cold. (나 감기 걸렸어.)
   B: Do you have a fever? (열이 나니?)
   G: No, but I have a cough and a runny nose.
      (아니, 하지만 기침을 하고 콧물이 나.)
   B: Oh, you should rest at home.
      (오, 너 집에서 쉬어야겠다.)
   Question: The girl has a fever and a cough.
      (소녀는 열이 나고 기침을 한다.)

2 W: Have some pizza. (피자 좀 먹으렴.)
   B: No, thank you. I have a stomachache.
      Should I go to the doctor?
      (아뇨, 괜찮아요. 저 배가 아파요. 병원에 가야 할까
      요?)
   W: No, take this medicine and rest. You'll be
      okay. (아니, 이 약을 먹고 쉬렴. 괜찮아질 거야.)
   B: Okay, Mom. (알겠어요, 엄마.)
   Question: The boy should see a doctor.
      (소년은 병원에 가야 한다.)

D Listen and mark.

1 B: Are you okay? What's wrong?
   (너 괜찮니? 어디 아프니?)
   G: I have a toothache. (이가 아파.)
   B: Oh, you should see a dentist.
      (오, 너 치과에 가야겠다.)
   G: Okay, I will. (응, 그럴게.)

2 B: Achoo! (에취!)
   G: Bless you. Do you have a cold?
      (저런, 몸조심해. 너 감기 걸렸니?)
   B: Yes, I do. (응.)
   G: Do you have a fever, too? (열도 나니?)
   B: No, but I have a sore throat.

(아니, 하지만 목이 아파.)
   G: Maybe you should see a doctor.
      (너 병원에 가야 할 것 같아.)

3 G: Mom, should I go to school?
   (엄마, 저 학교에 가야 해요?)
   W: Why? What's wrong? (왜 그러니? 어디 아프니?)
   G: I have a fever and a headache.
      (열이 나고 머리가 아파요.)
   W: Let me check. (pause) Oh, let's go to the
      doctor. (어디 보자. 이런, 병원에 가자.)
   G: Okay, Mom. (알겠어요, 엄마.)

P.37 LET'S SPEAK WITH BUDDY

Listen and say.

Mom: Jack, wake up! (Jack, 일어나거라!)
Jack: Mom, should I go to school?
      (엄마, 저 학교에 가야 해요?)

Mom: Why? What's wrong? (왜 그러니? 어디 아프니?)
Jack: I have a headache. (머리가 아파요.)

Mom: Do you have a fever, too? (열도 나니?)
Jack: Yes, I do. (네.)

Mom: Let's see a doctor after school.
      (방과 후에 병원에 가자.)

P.38~39 DICTATION

A Listen and write the letters.

1 cough (기침)
2 toothache (치통)
3 medicine (약)
4 sore throat (인후염(목 아픔))

B Listen and write the words.

1 Are you okay? What's wrong?
   (너 괜찮니? 어디 아프니?)
2 I have a cold. (나 감기 걸렸어.)
3 You should see a doctor. (너 병원에 가야겠다.)
4 Do you have a fever? (너 열이 나니?)
5 I have a headache. (나 머리가 아파.)

C Listen and fill in the blanks.

1 B: Are you okay? What's wrong?
   (너 괜찮니? 어디 아프니?)
   G: I have a toothache. (이가 아파.)
   B: Oh, you should see a dentist.
      (오, 너 치과에 가야겠다.)

2 G: Do you have a stomachache?
(너 배가 아프니?)
B: Yes, I do. (응.)
G: Maybe you should take some medicine.
(너 약을 좀 먹어야 할 것 같아.)

3 G: Achoo! (에취!)
B: Bless you! Do you have a cold?
(저런, 몸조심해! 너 감기 걸렸니?)
G: Yes, I have a cough and a headache.
(응, 기침이 나고 머리가 아파.)
B: Oh, you should rest at home.
(오, 너 집에서 쉬어야겠다.)

4 M: Are you okay? You don't look good.
(너 괜찮니? 안색이 안 좋아 보이는구나.)
G: I have a fever. (저 열이 나요.)
M: Do you have a sore throat, too?
(목도 아프니?)
G: No, but I have a runny nose.
(아뇨, 하지만 콧물이 나요.)
M: Let's go to the doctor. (병원에 가자.)

P.40~41 UNIT TEST

1 ⓐ headache (두통)   ⓑ toothache (치통)
ⓒ fever (열)   ⓓ runny nose (콧물)

2 ⓐ She has a sore throat. (그녀는 목이 아프다.)
ⓑ She has a headache. (그녀는 머리가 아프다.)
ⓒ He has a runny nose. (그는 콧물이 난다.)
ⓓ He has a cough. (그는 기침을 한다.)

3 W: Are you okay? You don't look good.
(너 괜찮니? 안색이 안 좋아 보이는구나.)
B: Mom, I have a stomachache.
(엄마, 저 배가 아파요.)
W: You should take some medicine.
(너 약을 좀 먹어야겠다.)
B: Okay, I will. (네, 그럴게요.)

4 G: Are you okay? What's wrong?
(너 괜찮니? 어디 아프니?)
B: I have a cough. (기침을 해.)
G: Do you have a fever, too? (열도 나니?)
B: _____
ⓐ No, I don't. (아니, 안 나.)
ⓑ You should rest at home. (너 집에서 쉬어야겠다.)
ⓒ Yes, it is. (응, 그래.)
ⓓ No, but I have a fever. (아니, 하지만 열이 나.)

5 G: Mom, should I go to school?
(엄마, 저 학교에 가야 해요?)

W: Why? What's wrong? (왜 그러니? 어디 아프니?)
G: I have a sore throat and a runny nose.
(목이 아프고 콧물이 나요.)
W: _____
ⓐ You shouldn't eat any more.
(더 이상 먹지 않는 게 좋겠다.)
ⓑ Okay, I will. (응, 그럴게.)
ⓒ Do you have a sore throat, too? (목도 아프니?)
ⓓ Let's go to the doctor. (병원에 가자.)

6 ⓐ B: Are you okay? What's wrong?
(너 괜찮니? 어디 아프니?)
G: I have a toothache. (이가 아파.)
ⓑ B: I have a headache. (저 머리가 아파요.)
W: Take this medicine. (이 약을 먹으렴.)
ⓒ B: Are you okay? You don't look good.
(너 괜찮니? 안색이 안 좋아 보여.)
G: Maybe you should see a doctor.
(너 병원에 가야 할 것 같아.)
ⓓ B: Do you have a cold? (너 감기 걸렸니?)
G: Yes, I have a cough and a runny nose.
(응, 기침을 하고 콧물이 나.)

7 B: Are you okay? What's wrong?
(너 괜찮니? 어디 아프니?)
G: I have a cold. (나 감기 걸렸어.)
B: Do you have a fever? (열이 나니?)
G: No, but I have a sore throat.
(아니, 하지만 목이 아파.)
B: Oh, you should take some medicine.
(오, 너 약을 좀 먹어야겠다.)
G: Okay, I will. (응, 그럴게.)

Question: What's wrong with the girl?
(소녀는 어디가 아픈가?)

8 B: Mom, should I go to school?
(엄마, 저 학교에 가야 해요?)
W: Why? What's wrong? (왜 그러니? 어디 아프니?)
B: I have a fever and a runny nose.
(열이 나고 콧물이 나요.)
W: Let me check. (*pause*) Oh, we should see a
doctor. (어디 보자. 오, 병원에 가야겠구나.)
B: Okay, Mom. (알겠어요, 엄마.)

Question: What should the boy do?
(소년은 무엇을 해야 하는가?)
ⓐ He should see a doctor. (그는 병원에 가야 한다.)
ⓑ He should take medicine. (그는 약을 먹어야 한다.)
ⓒ He should go to school. (그는 학교에 가야 한다.)
ⓓ He should rest at home. (그는 집에서 쉬어야 한다.)

UNIT 5 AT THE RESTAURANT

ANSWERS

P.42

P.43

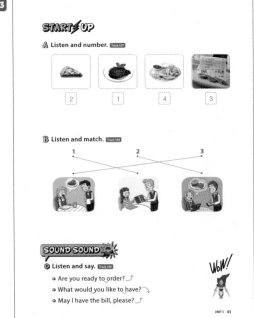

P.44

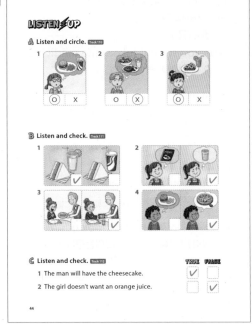

P.45

P.46~47 DICTATION

A 1 e, u   2 e, a   3 s, s   4 b, u, r

B 1 order   2 pie   3 like
4 drink   5 bill

C 1 ready, French, fries
2 would, like, steak, soda
3 dessert, menu, have, Anything

P.48~49 **UNIT TEST**

1 ⓓ   2 ⓒ   3 ⓐ   4 ⓒ
5 ⓒ   6 ⓓ   7 ⓑ   8 ⓓ

SCRIPTS & 해석

P.42 **ARE YOU READY?**

⚡ **Listen and number.**

1 **W**: Are you ready to order? (주문하시겠어요?)
M: Yes. I'll have the steak and the salad.
(네. 스테이크랑 샐러드로 할게요.)

2 **G**: Nick, what would you like to have?
(Nick, 뭐 먹을래?)
B: I want the apple pie. (난 사과 파이 먹을래.)

3 **W**: May I have the bill, please?
(계산서 좀 갖다 주시겠어요?)
M: Sure. Please wait a moment.
(물론이죠. 잠시만 기다려 주세요.)

⭐ **Listen and repeat.**

order (주문하다)   menu (메뉴, 식단표)
bill (계산서)   dessert (디저트, 후식)
steak (스테이크)   hamburger (햄버거)
French fries (감자튀김)   pie (파이)

P.43 **START UP**

A **Listen and number.**

1 steak (스테이크)
2 pie (파이)
3 bill (계산서)
4 French fries (감자튀김)

B **Listen and match.**

1 **G**: May I have the menu, please?
(메뉴판 좀 갖다 주시겠어요?)
M: Sure. (*pause*) Here you are.
(물론이죠. 여기 있습니다.)

2 **M**: Are you ready to order? (주문하시겠어요?)
G: Yes, I'll have a hamburger and French fries.
(네. 햄버거랑 감자튀김으로 할게요.)

3 **M**: Would you like some dessert?
(디저트 좀 드시겠어요?)
G: Yes, I'd like to have the apple pie.
(네, 사과 파이로 할게요.)

P.43 **SOUND SOUND**

🔊 **Listen and say.**

● Are you ready to order? (주문하시겠어요?)
● What would you like to have? (무엇을 드시겠어요?)
● May I have the bill, please?
(계산서 좀 갖다 주시겠어요?)

P.44~45 **LISTEN UP**

A **Listen and circle.**

1 **W**: Are you ready to order? (주문하시겠어요?)
G: Yes. I'll have a hamburger and French fries.
(네. 햄버거랑 감자튀김으로 할게요.)
W: Anything to drink? (마실 것은요?)
G: Soda, please. (탄산음료 주세요.)

2 **M**: What would you like to have?
(무엇을 드시겠어요?)
B: I'd like to have the steak and the salad.
(스테이크랑 샐러드로 할게요.)
M: Okay. Anything to drink?
(알겠습니다. 마실 것은요?)
B: No, that's all. Thank you.
(아뇨, 그게 다예요. 감사합니다.)

3 **M**: Are you ready to order? (주문하시겠어요?)
G: Yes, I'd like to have the apple pie.
(네, 사과 파이로 할게요.)
M: Anything to drink? (마실 것은요?)
G: Orange juice, please. (오렌지 주스 주세요.)

B **Listen and check.**

1 **W**: Are you ready to order? (주문하시겠어요?)
M: Yes, I want the chicken sandwich.
(네, 치킨 샌드위치로 할게요.)
W: Anything else? (다른 것은요?)
M: Lemonade, please. (레모네이드 주세요.)

2 **G**: Excuse me. (실례합니다.)
W: Yes. Can I help you? (네. 도와 드릴까요?)
G: May I have some water, please?
(물 좀 갖다 주시겠어요?)
W: Sure. Please wait a moment.
(물론이죠. 잠시만 기다려 주세요.)

3 **M**: Would you like some dessert?

(디저트 좀 드시겠어요?)

G: No, thank you. I'm full. May I have the bill, please?
(아뇨, 괜찮아요. 배불러요. 계산서 좀 갖다 주시겠어요?)

M: Of course. (*pause*) Here you are.
(물론이죠. 여기 있습니다.)

4 B: What would you like to have? (너 뭐 먹을래?)

G: I want a hamburger and French fries. How about you? (난 햄버거랑 감자튀김 먹을래. 너는?)

B: I'll have the cheese pizza.
(난 치즈 피자 먹을래.)

G: Okay. Let's order. (그래. 주문하자.)

Ⓒ Listen and check.

1 M: Excuse me. (실례합니다.)

W: Yes, sir. Can I help you?
(네, 손님. 도와 드릴까요?)

M: May I have the dessert menu?
(디저트 메뉴판 좀 갖다 주시겠어요?)

W: Sure. (*pause*) Here you are.
(물론이죠. 여기 있습니다.)

M: Oh, this cheesecake looks delicious. I'll have that.
(오, 이 치즈케이크가 맛있어 보이네요. 이것으로 할게요.)

W: Okay. Anything else?
(알겠습니다. 다른 것은요?)

M: No, that's all. Thank you.
(아뇨, 그게 다예요. 감사합니다.)

Question: The man will have the cheesecake.
(남자는 치즈케이크를 먹을 것이다.)

2 B: What would you like to have? (너 뭐 먹을래?)

G: I'll have the steak and the salad. How about you? (난 스테이크랑 샐러드 먹을래. 너는?)

B: I want the egg sandwich and an orange juice. (난 에그 샌드위치랑 오렌지 주스 먹을래.)

G: Oh, I'll have an orange juice, too.
(오, 나도 오렌지 주스 마실래.)

B: Okay. Let's order. (그래. 주문하자.)

Question: The girl doesn't want an orange juice.
(소녀는 오렌지 주스를 마시고 싶어 하지 않는다.)

Ⓓ Listen and mark.

1 W: Are you ready to order? (주문하시겠어요?)

B: Yes, I want the apple pie.
(네, 사과 파이로 할게요.)

W: Anything to drink? (마실 것은요?)

B: Do you have lemonade? (레모네이드 있나요?)

W: Yes, we do. (네, 있습니다.)

B: Lemonade, please. (레모네이드 주세요.)

W: Okay. Thank you. (알겠습니다. 감사합니다.)

2 G: Josh, what would you like to have?
(Josh, 뭐 먹을래?)

B: I'm still thinking. How about you?
(난 아직 생각 중이야. 너는?)

G: I'll have the steak. (난 스테이크 먹을래.)

B: Okay. I'll have the chicken.
(그래. 난 닭고기 먹을래.)

G: Good. Anything to drink? (좋아. 마실 것은?)

B: I'll have a soda. (난 탄산음료 마실래.)

P.45 LET'S SPEAK WITH BUDDY

🔵 Listen and say.

Tom: I'm hungry. (나 배고파.)
Jack: Let's go there! (저기 가자!)

Jack: What would you like to have? (너 뭐 먹을래?)
Tom: I want a hamburger and a soda.
(난 햄버거랑 탄산음료 먹을래.)

Waitress: Are you ready to order? (주문하시겠어요?)
Jack: Yes, we want two hamburgers and two sodas, please.
(네, 햄버거 두 개랑 탄산음료 두 개 주세요.)

Waitress: Sorry, but we only have desserts.
(죄송하지만, 디저트밖에 없어요.)

P.46~47 DICTATION

Ⓐ Listen and write the letters.

1 menu (메뉴, 식단표)
2 steak (스테이크)
3 dessert (디저트, 후식)
4 hamburger (햄버거)

Ⓑ Listen and write the words.

1 Are you ready to order? (주문하시겠어요?)
2 I'll have the apple pie. (난 사과 파이 먹을래.)
3 What would you like to have? (너 뭐 먹을래?)
4 Anything to drink? (마실 것은요?)
5 May I have the bill, please?
(계산서 좀 갖다 주시겠어요?)

Ⓒ Listen and fill in the blanks.

1 **W:** Are you ready to order? (주문하시겠어요?)

G: Yes. I'll have a hamburger and French fries.
(네. 햄버거랑 감자튀김으로 할게요.)

W: Anything to drink? (마실 것은요?)

G: Soda, please. (탄산음료 주세요.)

2 G: Josh, what would you like to have?
(Josh, 뭐 먹을래?)

B: I'm still thinking. How about you?
(난 아직 생각 중이야. 너는?)

G: I'll have the steak. (난 스테이크 먹을래.)

B: Okay. I'll have the chicken.
(그래. 난 닭고기 먹을래.)

G: Good. Anything to drink? (좋아. 마실 것은?)

B: I'll have a soda. (난 탄산음료 마실래.)

3 M: Excuse me. (실례합니다.)

W: Yes, sir. Can I help you?
(네, 손님. 도와 드릴까요?)

M: May I have the dessert menu?
(디저트 메뉴판 좀 갖다 주시겠어요?)

W: Sure. (pause) Here you are.
(물론이죠. 여기 있습니다.)

M: Oh, this cheesecake looks delicious. I'll
have that.
(오, 이 치즈케이크가 맛있어 보이네요. 이것으로 할
게요.)

W: Okay. Anything else?
(알겠습니다. 다른 것은요?)

M: No, that's all. Thank you.
(아뇨, 그게 다예요. 감사합니다.)

P.48~49 UNIT TEST

1 ⓐ dessert (디저트, 후식)   ⓑ steak (스테이크)
ⓒ French fries (감자튀김)   ⓓ hamburger (햄버거)

2 W: What will the woman say to the man?
(여자가 남자에게 할 말은 무엇인가?)

ⓐ May I have some water, please?
(물 좀 갖다 주시겠어요?)

ⓑ May I have the menu, please?
(메뉴판 좀 갖다 주시겠어요?)

ⓒ May I have the bill, please?
(계산서 좀 갖다 주시겠어요?)

ⓓ May I have the apple pie, please?
(사과 파이 좀 갖다 주시겠어요?)

3 B: What would you like to have? (너 뭐 먹을래?)

G: I'll have a hamburger and French fries. How
about you? (난 햄버거랑 감자튀김 먹을래. 너는?)

B: I'll have the steak. (난 스테이크 먹을래.)

4 W: Are you ready to order? (주문하시겠어요?)

G: Yes, I want the chicken. (네, 닭고기로 할게요.)

W: Anything to drink? (마실 것은요?)

G: _____

ⓐ No, thank you. I'm full.
(아뇨, 괜찮아요. 배불러요.)

ⓑ The chicken sandwich, please.
(치킨 샌드위치 주세요.)

ⓒ No, that's all. Thank you.
(아뇨, 그게 다예요. 감사합니다.)

ⓓ I'll have the cheesecake. (치즈케이크로 할게요.)

5 W: Excuse me. (실례합니다.)

M: Yes. Can I help you? (네. 도와 드릴까요?)

W: May I have the menu, please?
(메뉴판 좀 갖다 주시겠어요?)

M: _____

ⓐ Sorry, but we only have desserts.
(죄송하지만, 디저트밖에 없어요.)

ⓑ Anything to drink? (마실 것은요?)

ⓒ Sure. Please wait a moment.
(물론이죠. 잠시만 기다려 주세요.)

ⓓ I want the steak. (스테이크로 할게요.)

6 ⓐ W: Are you ready to order? (주문하시겠어요?)

M: Yes, I'll have the cheese pizza.
(네, 치즈 피자로 할게요.)

ⓑ W: Would you like some dessert?
(디저트 좀 드시겠어요?)

M: Yes. The apple pie, please.
(네. 사과 파이 주세요.)

ⓒ W: Do you have orange juice?
(오렌지 주스 있나요?)

M: Yes, we do. (네, 있습니다.)

ⓓ W: May I have the bill, please?
(계산서 좀 갖다 주시겠어요?)

M: What would you like to have?
(무엇을 드시겠어요?)

7 W: Would you like some dessert?
(디저트 좀 드시겠어요?)

B: No, thank you. I'm full. May I have some water,
please?
(아뇨, 괜찮아요. 배불러요. 물 좀 갖다 주시겠어요?)

W: Sure. Please wait a moment.
(물론이죠. 잠시만 기다려 주세요.)

Question: What will the woman do next?
(여자가 다음에 할 일은 무엇인가?)

8 B: What would you like to have? (너 뭐 먹을래?)

G: I'm still thinking. How about you?
(난 아직 생각 중이야. 너는?)

B: I want a hamburger and a soda.
　　(난 햄버거랑 탄산음료 먹을래.)
G: Okay. I'll have the steak.
　　(그래. 난 스테이크 먹을래.)
B: Anything else? (다른 것은?)
G: I want a salad, too. (난 샐러드도 먹을래.)
B: Okay, let's order. (그래, 주문하자.)

Question: What would the girl like to have?
　　　　　　(소녀는 무엇을 먹을 것인가?)

UNIT 6 SPECIAL DAYS

ANSWERS

P.50

P.51

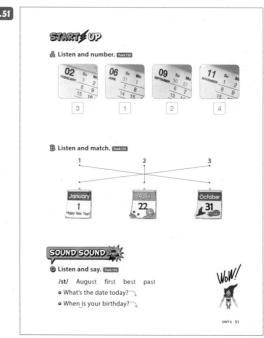

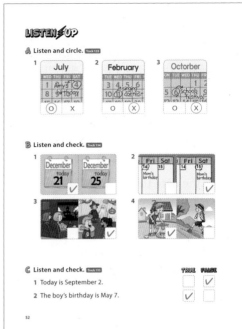

C
1 when, July
2 festival, October
3 April, Earth, Day
4 Christmas, December, plans

P.56~57 UNIT TEST

1 ⓑ   2 ⓓ   3 ⓐ   4 ⓑ
5 ⓒ   6 ⓓ   7 ⓒ   8 ⓐ

SCRIPTS & 해석

P.50 ARE YOU READY?

⚡ **Listen and number.**

1 B: What's the date today? (오늘 며칠이니?)
   G: It's November 11 (eleventh). (11월 11일이야.)

2 B: When is your birthday? (네 생일은 언제니?)
   G: It's June 3 (third). (6월 3일이야.)

⭐ **Listen and repeat.**

January (1월)	February (2월)	March (3월)
April (4월)	May (5월)	June (6월)
July (7월)	August (8월)	September (9월)
October (10월)	November (11월)	December (12월)

New Year's Day January 1 (first)
(새해 첫날 1월 1일)
Earth Day April 22 (twenty-second)
(지구의 날 4월 22일)
Halloween October 31 (thirty-first)
(할로윈 10월 31일)
Christmas December 25 (twenty-fifth)
(크리스마스 12월 25일)

P.51 START UP

A Listen and number.

1 June (6월)
2 September (9월)
3 February (2월)
4 November (11월)

B Listen and match.

1 G: What's the date today? (오늘 며칠이니?)
   B: It's October 31 (thirty-first). It's Halloween!
      (10월 31일이야. 할로윈이야!)

2 G: When is Earth Day? (지구의 날이 언제니?)
   B: It's April 22 (twenty-second). (4월 22일이야.)

P.54~55 DICTATION

A 1 l, y   2 n, u, a   3 s, t   4 v, e, m

B 1 date   2 birthday   3 September
    4 When   5 February

3 G: What's the date today? (오늘 며칠이니?)
B: It's January 1 (first). It's New Year's Day!
(1월 1일이야. 새해 첫날이야!)

P.51 SOUND SOUND

🔷 Listen and say.

/st/ August (8월)   first (첫째의)
best (최고의)   past (과거의)
○ What's the date today? (오늘 며칠이니?)
○ When is your birthday? (네 생일은 언제니?)

P.52~53 LISTEN UP

Ⓐ Listen and circle.

1 B: Amy, when is your birthday?
(Amy, 네 생일은 언제니?)
G: It's July 4 (fourth). (7월 4일이야.)
B: Oh, it's tomorrow! (오, 내일이구나!)

2 G: What's the date today? (오늘 며칠이니?)
B: It's February 11 (eleventh). My singing
contest is tomorrow.
(2월 11일이야. 노래 경연 대회가 내일이야.)
G: Good luck. (행운을 빌게.)

3 W: When is your school festival?
(너희 학교 축제는 언제니?)
B: It's next week, October 16 (sixteenth).
Can you come?
(다음 주예요, 10월 16일이요. 오실 수 있으세요?)
W: Sure. (물론이지.)

Ⓑ Listen and check.

1 G: Christmas is next week!
(크리스마스가 다음 주야!)
B: Oh, really? What's the date today?
(오, 정말? 오늘 며칠이니?)
G: It's December 21 (twenty-first).
(12월 21일이야.)
B: Do you have any special plans for
Christmas? (너 크리스마스에 특별한 계획 있니?)
G: Yes. I'll visit my grandmother.
(응. 난 할머니 댁을 방문할 거야.)

2 G: Is today August 15 (fifteenth)?
(오늘이 8월 15일이니?)
B: No, today is August 14 (fourteenth).
(아니, 오늘은 8월 14일이야.)
G: Tomorrow is Mom's birthday.
(내일이 엄마 생신이네.)

B: Really? Let's make dinner for her.
(정말? 엄마를 위해 저녁을 만들자.)

3 B: Do you have any special plans for
Halloween? (너 할로윈에 특별한 계획 있니?)
G: When is Halloween? (할로윈이 언제니?)
B: It's October 31 (thirty-first). How about
going to a Halloween party?
(10월 31일이야. 할로윈 파티에 가는 게 어때?)
G: That's a good idea. (좋은 생각이야.)

4 B: What's the date today? (오늘 며칠이니?)
G: It's April 22 (twenty-second). It's Earth Day.
(4월 22일이야. 지구의 날이야.)
B: What do people do on Earth Day?
(사람들은 지구의 날에 무엇을 하니?)
G: They pick up trash and save energy.
(쓰레기를 줍고 에너지를 절약해.)

Ⓒ Listen and check.

1 M: Kate, when is your school festival?
(Kate, 너희 학교 축제는 언제니?)
G: It's September 2 (second). (9월 2일이에요.)
M: Is today September 1 (first)?
(오늘이 9월 1일이니?)
G: Yes. Tomorrow is the school festival.
(네. 내일이 학교 축제예요.)
M: Okay, Mom and I will be there tomorrow.
(알겠다, 엄마와 내가 내일 거기 가야겠구나.)

Question: Today is September 2.
(오늘은 9월 2일이다.)

2 G: What's the date today? (오늘 며칠이니?)
B: It's May 4 (fourth). My birthday is next
week. (5월 4일이야. 내 생일이 다음 주야.)
G: Oh, really? When is it? (오, 정말? 언제인데?)
B: It's May 7 (seventh). (5월 7일이야.)
G: Do you have any special plans?
(특별한 계획 있니?)
B: Yes. I'll throw a party. Can you come?
(응. 파티를 열 거야. 너 올 수 있니?)
G: Sure. (물론이지.)

Question: The boy's birthday is May 7.
(소년의 생일은 5월 7일이다.)

Ⓓ Listen and write.

1 G: What's the date today? (오늘 며칠이니?)
B: It's December 31 (thirty-first).
(12월 31일이야.)
G: Then, tomorrow is New Year's Day!
(그럼, 내일이 새해 첫날이네!)

B: Right. Let's have a party. (맞아. 파티를 하자.)

G: Great. That sounds fun. (좋아. 재미있겠다.)

2 **B**: What's the date today? (오늘 며칠이니?)

G: It's April 22 (twenty-second). (4월 22일이야.)

B: Oh, it's Earth Day. Let's pick up trash.
(오, 지구의 날이네. 쓰레기를 줍자.)

G: That's a good idea. (좋은 생각이야.)

P.53 **LET'S SPEAK WITH BUDDY**

🔷 **Listen and say.**

Jack: What's the date today? (오늘 며칠이니?)

Tom: It's June 1 (first). (6월 1일이야.)

Jack: Today is Jenny's birthday! Let's have a
surprise party for her.
(오늘이 Jenny의 생일이야! 그녀를 위해 깜짝 파티
를 열자.)

Jack, Tom, other friends: Happy birthday, Jenny!
(생일 축하해, Jenny!)

Jenny: What? Today isn't my birthday.
(뭐? 오늘은 내 생일이 아니야.)

Jack: When is your birthday? (네 생일은 언제인데?)

Jenny: It's July 1 (first). (7월 1일이야.)

P.54~55 **DICTATION**

Ⓐ **Listen and write the letters.**

1 July (7월)

2 January (1월)

3 August (8월)

4 November (11월)

Ⓑ **Listen and write the words.**

1 What's the date today? (오늘 며칠이니?)

2 My birthday is next week. (내 생일은 다음 주야.)

3 Is today September 1 (first)?
(오늘이 9월 1일이니?)

4 When is Halloween? (할로윈이 언제니?)

5 Today is February 14 (fourteenth).
(오늘은 2월 14일이야.)

Ⓒ **Listen and fill in the blanks.**

1 **B**: Amy, when is your birthday?
(Amy, 네 생일은 언제니?)

G: It's July 4 (fourth). (7월 4일이야.)

B: Oh, it's tomorrow! (오, 내일이구나!)

2 **W**: When is your school festival?
(너희 학교 축제는 언제니?)

B: It's next week, October 16 (sixteenth).
Can you come?
(다음 주예요, 10월 16일이요. 오실 수 있으세요?)

W: Sure. (물론이지.)

3 **B**: What's the date today? (오늘 며칠이니?)

G: It's April 22 (twenty-second). (4월 22일이야.)

B: Oh, it's Earth Day. Let's pick up trash.
(오, 지구의 날이네. 쓰레기를 줍자.)

G: That's a good idea. (좋은 생각이야.)

4 **G**: Christmas is next week!
(크리스마스가 다음 주야!)

B: Oh, really? What's the date today?
(오, 정말? 오늘 며칠이니?)

G: It's December 21 (twenty-first).
(12월 21일이야.)

B: Do you have any special plans for Christmas?
(너 크리스마스에 특별한 계획 있니?)

G: Yes. I'll visit my grandmother.
(응. 난 할머니 댁을 방문할 거야.)

P.56~57 **UNIT TEST**

1 ⓐ New Year's Day (새해 첫날)

ⓑ Earth Day (지구의 날)

ⓒ Halloween (할로윈)

ⓓ Christmas (크리스마스)

2 ⓐ It's September 6 (sixth). (9월 6일이다.)

ⓑ It's November 6 (sixth). (11월 6일이다.)

ⓒ It's September 16 (sixteenth). (9월 16일이다.)

ⓓ It's November 16 (sixteenth). (11월 16일이다.)

3 **G**: What's the date today? (오늘 며칠이니?)

B: It's October 31 (thirty-first). It's Halloween.
(10월 31일이야. 할로윈이야.)

G: Do you have any special plans?
(특별한 계획 있니?)

B: Yes, I'll go to a Halloween party.
(응, 할로윈 파티에 갈 거야.)

4 ⓐ **W**: Is today August 13 (thirteenth)?
(오늘이 8월 13일이니?)

B: Yes, it is. (네, 맞아요.)

ⓑ **W**: When is your school festival?
(너희 학교 축제는 언제니?)

B: It's October 13 (thirteenth).
(10월 13일이에요.)

ⓒ **W**: Do you have any special plans?
(특별한 계획 있니?)

B: No. Let's go to the festival. (아뇨. 축제에 가요.)

27

ⓓ W: What's the date today? (오늘 며칠이니?)
   B: It's October 10 (tenth). (10월 10일이에요.)

5　B: What's the date today? (오늘 며칠이니?)
　　ⓐ It's my birthday. (내 생일이야.)
　　ⓑ Oh, it's tomorrow. (오, 내일이야.)
　　ⓒ It's May 15 (fifteenth). (5월 15일이야.)
　　ⓓ Let's have a party. (파티를 열자.)

6　ⓐ B: When is your birthday? (네 생일은 언제니?)
　　　　G: It's July 1 (first). (7월 1일이야.)
　　ⓑ B: What's the date today? (오늘 며칠이니?)
　　　　G: It's April 22 (twenty-second), Earth Day.
　　　　　 (4월 22일, 지구의 날이야.)
　　ⓒ B: Do you have any special plans for
　　　　Christmas? (너 크리스마스에 특별한 계획 있니?)
　　　　G: Yes. I'll throw a party. (응. 난 파티를 열 거야.)
　　ⓓ B: Is today January 6 (sixth)?
　　　　　 (오늘이 1월 6일이니?)
　　　　G: Yes, tomorrow is February 7 (seventh).
　　　　　 (응, 내일이 2월 7일이야.)

7　B: Is today March 11 (eleventh)?
　　　 (오늘이 3월 11일이니?)
　　G: No, today is March 12 (twelfth).
　　　 (아니, 오늘은 3월 12일이야.)
　　B: Oh, tomorrow is Dad's birthday.
　　　 (오, 내일이 아빠 생신이네.)
　　G: Really? Is his birthday March 13 (thirteenth)?
　　　 (정말? 아빠 생신이 3월 13일이야?)
　　B: Yes. Let's make dinner for him.
　　　 (응. 아빠를 위해 저녁을 만들자.)
　　G: That's a good idea. (좋은 생각이야.)

　　Question: When is Dad's birthday?
　　　　　　　 (아빠의 생신은 언제인가?)

8　G: Christmas is next week! (크리스마스가 다음 주야!)
　　B: Oh, really? What's the date today?
　　　 (오, 정말? 오늘 며칠이니?)
　　G: It's December 20 (twentieth). (12월 20일이야.)
　　B: Do you have any special plans for Christmas?
　　　 (너 크리스마스에 특별한 계획 있니?)
　　G: No. Let's watch a movie together.
　　　 (아니. 함께 영화 보자.)
　　B: That sounds fun. (재미있겠다.)

　　Question: Today is December 20.
　　　　　　　 (오늘은 12월 20일이다.)

REVIEW TEST 2　UNITS 4~6

1 ⓓ	2 ⓒ	3 ⓑ	4 ⓑ	5 ⓒ
6 ⓓ	7 ⓐ	8 ⓒ	9 ⓑ	10 ⓓ

1　ⓐ fever (열)
　　ⓑ toothache (치통)
　　ⓒ sore throat (인후통(목 아픔))
　　ⓓ stomachache (복통)

2　ⓐ New Year's Day (새해 첫날)
　　ⓑ Earth Day (지구의 날)
　　ⓒ Halloween (할로윈)
　　ⓓ Christmas (크리스마스)

3　G: Excuse me. (실례합니다.)
　　M: Yes. Can I help you? (네. 도와 드릴까요?)
　　G: May I have the menu, please?
　　　 (메뉴판 좀 갖다 주시겠어요?)
　　M: Sure. Please wait a moment.
　　　 (물론이죠. 잠시만 기다려 주세요.)

4　B: What's the date today? (오늘 며칠이니?)
　　G: It's July 4 (fourth). (7월 4일이야.)
　　B: Oh, Amy's birthday is next week.
　　　 (오, Amy의 생일이 다음 주야.)
　　G: Really? When is it? (정말? 언제인데?)
　　B: _____
　　ⓐ It's July 4 (fourth). (7월 4일이야.)
　　ⓑ It's July 9 (ninth). (7월 9일이야.)
　　ⓒ Let's throw a party. (파티를 열자.)
　　ⓓ It's Amy's birthday. (Amy의 생일이야.)

5　G: Are you okay? What's wrong?
　　　 (너 괜찮니? 어디 아프니?)
　　B: I have a cold. (감기 걸렸어.)
　　G: Do you have a runny nose? (콧물이 나니?)
　　B: No, but I have a cough and a sore throat.
　　　 (아니, 하지만 기침이 나고 목이 아파.)
　　G: _____
　　ⓐ Let's go to the dentist. (치과에 가자.)
　　ⓑ Should I go to the doctor? (나 병원에 가야 할까?)
　　ⓒ You should take medicine. (너 약을 먹어야겠다.)
　　ⓓ I have a runny nose, too. (나도 콧물이 나.)

6　ⓐ B: What would you like to have? (너 뭐 먹을래?)
　　　　G: I want the steak and an orange juice.
　　　　　 (난 스테이크랑 오렌지 주스 먹을래.)
　　ⓑ B: Are you okay? You don't look good.
　　　　　 (너 괜찮니? 안색이 안 좋아 보여.)
　　　　G: I have a fever and a headache.
　　　　　 (나 열이 나고 머리가 아파.)

ⓒ **B**: What's the date today? (오늘 며칠이니?)

   G: It's October 31 (thirty-first). It's Halloween.
   (10월 31일이야. 할로윈이야.)

ⓓ **W**: Are you ready to order? (주문하시겠어요?)

   G: Yes. Here you are. (네. 여기 있습니다.)

7 ⓐ **B**: Maybe you should see a doctor.
   (너 병원에 가야 할 것 같아.)

   G: Okay, take this medicine. (그래, 이 약을 먹어.)

ⓑ **B**: Is today March 17 (seventeenth)?
   (오늘이 3월 17일이니?)

   G: Yes, it is. (응, 그래.)

ⓒ **W**: Would you like some dessert?
   (디저트 좀 드시겠어요?)

   G: Yes. The apple pie, please.
   (네. 사과 파이 주세요.)

ⓓ **B**: When is Earth Day? (지구의 날이 언제니?)

   G: It's April 22 (twenty-second). (4월 22일이야.)

8 **W**: Are you ready to order? (주문하시겠어요?)

   B: Yes, I'd like to have the steak and the French
   fries. (네, 스테이크랑 감자튀김으로 할게요.)

   W: Anything to drink? (마실 것은요?)

   B: Soda, please. (탄산음료 주세요.)

   W: Okay, thank you. (네, 감사합니다.)

   Question: Which one is the boy's food?
   (소년의 음식은 어느 것인가?)

9 **G**: Dad, is today September 18 (eighteenth)?
   (아빠, 오늘이 9월 18일이에요?)

   M: No, it's September 19 (nineteenth).
   (아니, 9월 19일이란다.)

   G: Oh, the school festival is next week,
   September 26 (twenty-sixth). Can you come?
   (오, 학교 축제가 다음 주예요, 9월 26일이요. 오실 수
   있으세요?)

   M: Sure. Mom and I will be there.
   (물론이지. 엄마와 내가 거기 가야겠구나.)

   Question: What is the date today?
   (오늘은 며칠인가?)

10 G: Mom, should I go to school?
   (엄마, 저 학교에 가야 해요?)

   W: Why? What's wrong? (왜 그러니? 어디 아프니?)

   G: I have a fever. (열이 나요.)

   W: Do you have a cough, too? (기침도 나니?)

   G: No, but I have a headache.
   (아뇨, 하지만 머리가 아파요.)

   W: Let's go to the doctor. (병원에 가자.)

   Question: The girl has a fever and a headache.
   (소녀는 열이 나고 머리가 아프다.)

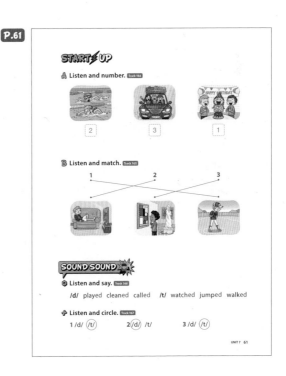

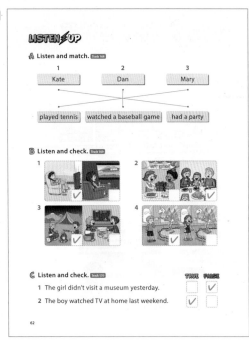

P.62

LISTEN UP

A Listen and match. Track 168

1 Kate 2 Dan 3 Mary

played tennis　watched a baseball game　had a party

B Listen and check. Track 169

1 ✓ 　2 ✓
3 ✓ 　4 ✓

C Listen and check. Track 170

	TRUE	FALSE
1 The girl didn't visit a museum yesterday.		✓
2 The boy watched TV at home last weekend.	✓	

62

P.63

D Listen and number in time order. Track 171

2 → 3 → 1

LET'S SPEAK WITH BUDDY

Listen and say. Track 172

Hi, Jenny! How was your vacation?
It was great!
What did you do?
I took a trip to Europe. There were many beautiful sights.
Wow, cool! Did you take photos?
Sure. Here, you can look at them.
Beautiful...

❖Listen again and repeat.

UNIT 7　63

P.64~65 # DICTATION

A 1 had　2 watched　3 took　4 played

B 1 do　2 was　3 visited　4 went　5 Did

C 1 go, watched
2 didn't, visited, Did, took
3 How, was, went, played, had

P.66~67 # UNIT TEST

1 ⓑ　2 ⓓ　3 ⓒ　4 ⓓ
5 ⓐ　6 ⓒ　7 ⓒ　8 ⓓ

SCRIPTS & 해석

P.60 ## ARE YOU READY?

⚡ Listen and number.

1 B: What did you do yesterday? (너 어제 뭐 했니?)
G: I visited a museum. (박물관을 방문했어.)

2 B: How was your weekend? (주말 어땠니?)
G: It was a lot of fun. I took a trip with my family.
(정말 재미있었어. 나는 가족과 여행을 갔어.)

⭐ Listen and repeat.

played baseball (야구를 했다)
watched TV (TV를 보았다)
visited a museum (박물관을 방문했다)
went swimming (수영하러 갔다)
had a party (파티를 열었다)
took a trip (여행을 갔다)

P.61 ## START UP

A Listen and number.

1 had a party (파티를 열었다)
2 went swimming (수영하러 갔다)
3 took a trip (여행을 갔다)

B Listen and match.

1 G: What did you do last Sunday?
(너 지난 일요일에 뭐 했니?)
B: I played baseball with my friends.
(친구들과 야구를 했어.)

2 G: Did you go to a movie yesterday?
(너 어제 영화 보러 갔었니?)
B: No, I didn't. I just watched TV at home.
(아니, 안 갔어. 나는 그냥 집에서 TV를 봤어.)

3 G: How was your trip? (여행 어땠니?)
B: It was great. I visited a lot of museums.
(멋졌어. 나는 많은 박물관을 방문했어.)

30

SOUND SOUND

🔵 **Listen and say.**

/d/ played (놀았다)   cleaned (청소했다)
  called (불렀다)
/t/ watched (보았다)   jumped (뛰어올랐다)
  walked (걸었다)

➕ **Listen and circle.**

  1 watched   **2** cleaned   **3** walked

LISTEN UP

Ⓐ **Listen and match.**

1 B: Kate, what did you do last Saturday?
(Kate, 너 지난 토요일에 뭐 했니?)
G: It was my mom's birthday. I had a surprise party for her.
(엄마 생신이었어. 나는 엄마를 위해 깜짝 파티를 열었어.)

2 G: Dan, did you play baseball last weekend?
(Dan, 너 지난 주말에 야구 했니?)
B: No, I didn't. I watched a baseball game with my father.
(아니, 안 했어. 나는 아빠와 야구 경기를 봤어.)

3 B: Mary, what did you do yesterday?
(Mary, 너 어제 뭐 했니?)
G: I played tennis with my friend. It was fun.
(친구와 테니스를 쳤어. 재미있었어.)

Ⓑ **Listen and check.**

1 B: What did you do yesterday? (너 어제 뭐 했니?)
G: I watched a movie at home.
(집에서 영화를 봤어.)
B: How was the movie? (영화는 어땠니?)
G: It was boring. (지루했어.)

2 B: Did you go to Tony's party last Friday?
(너 지난 금요일에 Tony의 파티에 갔었니?)
G: No, I didn't. (아니, 안 갔어.)
B: Then, what did you do? (그럼, 뭐 했니?)
G: I had dinner with my family.
(나는 가족과 저녁을 먹었어.)

3 G: How was your weekend? (주말 어땠니?)
B: It was fun. I visited my friend.
(재미있었어. 나는 친구를 방문했어.)
G: What did you do together? (같이 뭐 했는데?)
B: We went camping. (우리는 캠핑을 갔었어.)

4 B: How was your vacation? (방학 어땠니?)

G: It was great. I visited my grandma. We went swimming together. How about your vacation?
(멋졌어. 나는 할머니 댁을 방문했어. 우리는 함께 수영하러 갔었어. 너는 방학 어땠니?)
B: My family took a trip to Europe. We visited a lot of museums.
(우리 가족은 유럽으로 여행을 갔었어. 우리는 많은 박물관을 방문했어.)
G: Wow, cool! (와, 멋지다!)

Ⓒ **Listen and check.**

1 G: Did you go to Sam's birthday party?
(너 Sam의 생일 파티에 갔었니?)
B: Yes, I did. I didn't see you there.
(응, 갔어. 거기서 너를 보지 못했는데.)
G: I was busy yesterday. (나는 어제 바빴어.)
B: What did you do? (뭐 했니?)
G: I visited a museum. (박물관을 방문했어.)
B: Did you have fun? (재미있었니?)
G: Yes, I did. I took a lot of photos.
(응, 재미있었어. 나는 사진을 많이 찍었어.)

Question: The girl didn't visit a museum yesterday.
(소녀는 어제 박물관을 방문하지 않았다.)

2 B: What did you do last weekend?
(너 지난 주말에 뭐 했니?)
G: I went to the festival. (축제에 갔었어.)
B: Cool! How was it? (멋지다! 어땠니?)
G: It was very fun. I watched the fireworks. There were a lot of people. How about you?
(정말 재미있었어. 나는 불꽃놀이를 봤어. 사람들이 많았어. 너는?)
B: I just watched TV at home.
(나는 그냥 집에서 TV를 봤어.)

Question: The boy watched TV at home last weekend.
(소년은 지난 주말에 집에서 TV를 보았다.)

Ⓓ **Listen and number in time order.**

G: How was your weekend? (주말 어땠니?)
B: It was great. I was at my uncle's house.
(좋았어. 나는 삼촌 댁에 있었어.)
G: What did you do there? (거기서 뭐 했니?)
B: I went swimming with my cousins on Saturday. (토요일에는 사촌들과 수영하러 갔었어.)
G: What about on Sunday? (일요일에는?)
B: We played baseball in the morning and then we had lunch together.

(우리는 아침에는 야구를 했고, 그다음엔 함께 점심을 먹었어.)

P.63 LET'S SPEAK WITH BUDDY

🎧 Listen and say.

Ann: Hi, Jenny! How was your vacation?
(안녕, Jenny! 방학 어땠니?)

Jenny: It was great! (멋졌어!)

Ann: What did you do? (뭐 했니?)

Jenny: I took a trip to Europe. There were many beautiful sights.
(유럽으로 여행을 갔었어. 아름다운 명소들이 많았어.)

Ann: Wow, cool! Did you take photos?
(와, 멋진데! 사진은 찍었니?)

Jenny: Sure. Here, you can look at them.
(물론이지. 여기, 사진들을 볼 수 있어.)

Ann: Beautiful... (예쁘다…)

P.64~65 DICTATION

Ⓐ Listen and write the words.

1 had a party (파티를 열었다)
2 watched TV (TV를 보았다)
3 took a trip (여행을 갔다)
4 played baseball (야구를 했다)

Ⓑ Listen and write the words.

1 What did you do yesterday? (너 어제 뭐 했니?)
2 How was your trip? (여행 어땠니?)
3 I visited a lot of museums.
(나는 많은 박물관을 방문했어.)
4 I went swimming with my father.
(나는 아빠와 수영하러 갔어.)
5 Did you play baseball last weekend?
(너 지난 주말에 야구 했니?)

Ⓒ Listen and fill in the blanks.

1 G: Did you go to a movie yesterday?
(너 어제 영화 보러 갔었니?)
B: No, I didn't. I just watched TV at home.
(아니, 안 갔어. 나는 그냥 집에서 TV를 봤어.)

2 G: Did you go to Sam's birthday party?
(너 Sam의 생일 파티에 갔었니?)
B: Yes, I did. I didn't see you there.
(응, 갔어. 거기서 너를 보지 못했는데.)
G: I was busy yesterday. (나 어제 바빴어.)

B: What did you do? (뭐 했니?)
G: I visited a museum. (박물관을 방문했어.)
B: Did you have fun? (재미있었니?)
G: Yes, I did. I took a lot of photos.
(응, 재미있었어. 나는 사진을 많이 찍었어.)

3 G: How was your weekend? (주말 어땠니?)
B: It was great. I was at my uncle's house.
(좋았어. 나는 삼촌 댁에 있었어.)
G: What did you do there? (거기서 뭐 했니?)
B: I went swimming with my cousins on
Saturday. (토요일에는 사촌들과 수영하러 갔었어.)
G: What about on Sunday? (일요일에는?)
B: We played baseball in the morning and
then we had lunch together.
(우리는 아침에는 야구를 했고, 그다음엔 함께 점심을
먹었어.)

P.66~67 UNIT TEST

1 ⓐ had a party (파티를 열었다)
ⓑ took a trip (여행을 갔다)
ⓒ watched TV (TV를 보았다)
ⓓ played baseball (야구를 했다)

2 ⓐ She went swimming yesterday.
(그녀는 어제 수영하러 갔다.)
ⓑ She played tennis yesterday.
(그녀는 어제 테니스를 쳤다.)
ⓒ She watched a movie yesterday.
(그녀는 어제 영화를 봤다.)
ⓓ She visited a museum yesterday.
(그녀는 어제 박물관을 방문했다.)

3 G: How was your vacation? (방학 어땠니?)
B: It was boring. (지루했어.)
G: What did you do? (뭐 했니?)
B: I just watched TV at home.
(그냥 집에서 TV를 봤어.)

4 G: I was busy yesterday. (나는 어제 바빴어.)
B: What did you do? (뭐 했니?)
G: _____
ⓐ Did you go to a movie? (너 영화 보러 갔었니?)
ⓑ What about on Sunday? (일요일에는?)
ⓒ There were a lot of people. (사람들이 많았어.)
ⓓ I had a surprise party for my mom.
(나는 엄마를 위해 깜짝 파티를 열었어.)

5 G: What did you do last weekend?
(너 지난 주말에 뭐 했니?)
B: I took a trip with my family.

(가족과 여행을 갔어.)

G: How was your trip? (여행은 어땠니?)

B: _____

ⓐ It was a lot of fun. (정말 재미있었어.)

ⓑ I watched TV at home. (나는 집에서 TV를 봤어.)

ⓒ It was my dad's birthday. (아빠의 생신이었어.)

ⓓ I was busy last Monday.
   (나는 지난 월요일에 바빴어.)

6 ⓐ **G**: What did you do yesterday? (너 어제 뭐 했니?)
   B: I went to the festival. (축제에 갔었어.)
   ⓑ **G**: How was the movie? (그 영화 어땠니?)
   B: It was boring. (지루했어.)
   ⓒ **G**: Did you play baseball last Sunday?
      (너 지난 일요일에 야구 했니?)
   B: Yes, I watched a baseball game with my
      father. (응, 나는 아빠랑 야구 경기를 봤어.)
   ⓓ **G**: What did you do last weekend?
      (너 지난 주말에 뭐 했니?)
   B: I visited my grandmother.
      (할머니 댁을 방문했어.)

7 **G**: Did you go to the festival yesterday?
      (너 어제 축제에 갔었니?)
   B: Yes, I did. I didn't see you there.
      (응, 갔어. 거기서 너를 보지 못했는데.)
   G: I was at my uncle's house. (나는 삼촌 댁에 있었어.)
   B: What did you do there? (거기서 뭐 했니?)
   G: It was my uncle's birthday. We had a party for
      him.
      (삼촌의 생신이었어. 우리는 삼촌을 위해 파티를 열었어.)

   Question: What did the girl do yesterday?
      (소녀는 어제 무엇을 했는가?)

8 **B**: Sue, how was your weekend? (Sue, 주말 어땠니?)
   G: It was fun. I went swimming with my sister.
      How about you?
      (재미있었어. 나는 언니와 수영하러 갔어. 너는?)
   B: I visited my friend. (나는 친구를 방문했어.)
   G: What did you do together? (같이 뭐 했는데?)
   B: We played baseball. (우리는 야구를 했어.)
   G: Did you have fun? (재미있었니?)
   B: Yes, I did. (응, 재미있었어.)

   Question: The boy played baseball last weekend.
      (소년은 지난 주말에 <u>야구를 했다</u>.)

UNIT 8 PHONE CALLS

ANSWERS

P.68

P.69

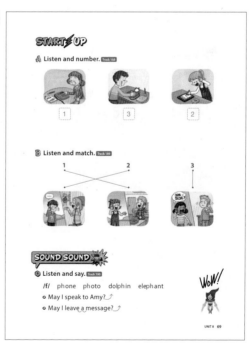

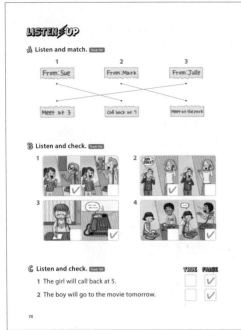

P.72~73 DICTATION

A 1 back 2 hang 3 hold 4 answer

B 1 speak 2 wrong 3 phone
4 message 5 call

C 1 Speaking, calling
2 May, leave, meet
3 This, is, call, back
4 speak, hang, up, Hold, on

P.74~75 UNIT TEST

1 ⓓ 2 ⓑ 3 ⓒ 4 ⓑ
5 ⓒ 6 ⓒ 7 ⓐ 8 ⓓ

SCRIPTS & 해석

P.68 ARE YOU READY?

⚡ **Listen and number.**

1 (*Phone rings.*)
   W: Hello? (여보세요?)
   B: Hello? May I speak to Amy?
      (여보세요? Amy와 통화할 수 있을까요?)
   W: Who's calling, please? (누구세요?)
   B: This is Mike. (마이크예요.)
   W: Hold on, please. (잠시만 기다리렴.)

2 (*Phone rings.*)
   W: Hello? (여보세요?)
   B: Hello? May I speak to Linda?
      (여보세요? Linda와 통화할 수 있을까요?)
   W: She's not at home. (그녀는 집에 없단다.)
   B: May I leave a message? (메모 남겨도 될까요?)
   W: Sure. (물론이지.)

⭐ **Listen and repeat.**

answer the phone (전화를 받다)
hold on (전화를 끊지 않고 기다리다)
leave a message (메모를 남기다)
call back (다시 전화를 하다)
hang up (전화를 끊다)
have the wrong number (전화를 잘못 걸다)

P.69 START UP

A **Listen and number.**

1 call back (다시 전화를 하다)
2 leave a message (메모를 남기다)
3 hang up (전화를 끊다)

B **Listen and match.**

1 G: May I speak to Josh?
   (Josh와 통화할 수 있을까요?)
   B: Speaking. Who's calling, please?

34

(전데요. 누구세요?)

G: This is Sue. (나 Sue야.)

2 **B**: May I speak to Kate?
(Kate와 통화할 수 있을까요?)

W: Sure. Hold on, please. (*pause*) Kate, it's for you! (그래. 잠시만 기다리렴. Kate, 네 전화구나!)

3 **G**: May I speak to Joe? (Joe와 통화할 수 있을까요?)

B: Sorry, but you have the wrong number.
(죄송하지만, 전화 잘못 거셨어요.)

G: Oh, I'm sorry. (오, 죄송해요.)

P.69 SOUND SOUND

◉ **Listen and say.**

/f/ phone (전화(기)) photo (사진)
dolphin (돌고래) elephant (코끼리)

◦ May I speak to Amy? (Amy와 통화할 수 있을까요?)
◦ May I leave a message? (메모 남겨도 될까요?)

P.70~71 LISTEN UP

A **Listen and match.**

1 **G**: This is Sue. May I leave a message?
(저 Sue인데요. 메모 남겨도 될까요?)

M: Sure. (물론이지.)

G: Please tell Joe to call me back at 7.
(Joe에게 7시에 저한테 전화해 달라고 전해주세요.)

2 **B**: This is Mark. May I leave a message?
(나 Mark인데. 메모 남겨도 될까?)

G: Sure. Go ahead. (네. 말씀하세요.)

B: Please tell your sister to meet me at the park. (너희 언니에게 공원에서 만나자고 전해줘.)

3 **G**: This is Julie. May I leave a message?
(저 Julie인데요. 메모 남겨도 될까요?)

W: Sure. (물론이지.)

G: Please tell Peter to meet me at 3, not 2.
(Peter에게 2시가 아니라 3시에 만나자고 전해주세요.)

B **Listen and check.**

1 **G**: Hello? May I speak to Tim?
(여보세요? Tim과 통화할 수 있을까요?)

B: Speaking. Who's calling? (전데요. 누구세요?)

G: This is Olivia. (나 Olivia야.)

B: Hi, Olivia. What's up?
(안녕, Olivia. 무슨 일이야?)

2 **B**: Hello? May I speak to Kate?

(여보세요? Kate와 통화할 수 있을까요?)

W: I'm sorry. You have the wrong number.
(미안하지만, 전화를 잘못 건 것 같구나.)

B: Oh, really? Isn't this 354-3562?
(오, 정말요? 거기 354-3562 아닌가요?)

W: No, it isn't. (아닌데.)

B: Oh, I'm sorry. (오, 죄송해요.)

3 **G**: This is Jessica. I can't answer the phone right now. Please leave a message. (*beep*)
(Jessica입니다. 지금은 전화를 받을 수 없습니다. 메모를 남겨주세요.)

B: Hi, Jessica. This is Kevin. Please call me back after school.
(안녕, Jessica. 나 Kevin이야. 방과 후에 나한테 전화해줘.)

4 **G**: Hello? May I speak to Ben?
(여보세요? Ben과 통화할 수 있을까요?)

B: My brother is not at home right now.
(동생은 지금 집에 없는데.)

G: Okay. I'll call him back.
(알겠어요. 제가 다시 전화할게요.)

B: Oh, don't hang up. He's home now. Hold on, please. (*pause*) Ben, it's for you!
(오, 끊지 마. 그가 지금 집에 왔어. 잠시만 기다리렴. Ben, 네 전화야!)

C **Listen and check.**

1 (*Phone rings.*)

W: Hello? (여보세요?)

G: Hello? May I speak to Sam?
(여보세요? Sam과 통화할 수 있을까요?)

W: He's not at home right now. Who's calling?
(그는 지금 집에 없단다. 누구니?)

G: This is Mary, Sam's friend. May I leave a message?
(저 Sam의 친구 Mary인데요. 메모 남겨도 될까요?)

W: Sure. (물론이지.)

G: Please tell him to call me back at 5.
(Sam에게 5시에 저한테 전화해 달라고 전해주세요.)

W: Okay. (그래.)

Question: The girl will call back at 5.
(소녀는 5시에 다시 전화할 것이다.)

2 **G**: This is Lily. I can't answer the phone right now. Please leave a message. (*beep*)
(Lily입니다. 지금은 전화를 받을 수 없습니다. 메모를 남겨주세요.)

B: Hi, Lily. This is Ben. I'm sorry, but I can't go to the movie tomorrow. I'm sick, so I will

35

stay at home tomorrow. Call me later. Bye.
(안녕, Lily. 나 Ben이야. 미안하지만, 난 내일 영화 보러 갈 수 없어. 몸이 아파서 내일 집에 있을 거야. 나중에 전화해줘. 안녕.)

Question: The boy will go to the movie tomorrow.
(소년은 내일 영화를 보러 갈 것이다.)

⒟ Listen and number in order.

(Phone rings.)

W: Hello? (여보세요?)

B: Hello? This is Peter. May I speak to Kate?
(여보세요? 저 Peter인데요. Kate와 통화할 수 있을까요?)

W: Hi, Peter! She's not at home right now.
(안녕, Peter! 그녀는 지금 집에 없단다.)

B: May I leave a message? (메모 남겨도 될까요?)

W: Sure. (물론이지.)

B: Please tell her to call me back.
(그녀에게 저한테 전화해 달라고 전해주세요.)

W: Okay. Oh, wait. She's home now. Hold on, please. (pause)
(그래. 오, 기다리렴. 그녀가 지금 집에 왔구나. 잠시만 기다리렴.)

G: Hello? This is Kate. What's up?
(여보세요? 나 Kate야. 무슨 일이야?)

B: Can we meet at 3 tomorrow?
(내일 3시에 만날 수 있니?)

G: Sure. See you tomorrow. (그럼. 내일 보자.)

P.71 LET'S SPEAK WITH BUDDY

◉ Listen and say.

(Phone rings.)

Kevin: Hello? (여보세요?)

Tom: Hello? May I speak to Ann?
(여보세요? Ann과 통화할 수 있니?)

Kevin: She's not here right now. Who's calling?
(누나는 지금 여기 없는데요. 누구세요?)

Tom: This is Tom. (난 Tom이야.)

Tom: May I leave a message? (메모 남겨도 될까?)

Ann: Hello, this is Ann. I'll call you back.
(여보세요, 나 Ann이야. 내가 다시 전화할게.)

P.72~73 DICTATION

Ⓐ Listen and write the words.

1 call back (다시 전화를 하다)

2 hang up (전화를 끊다)
3 hold on (전화를 끊지 않고 기다리다)
4 answer the phone (전화를 받다)

Ⓑ Listen and write the words.

1 May I speak to Amy? (Amy와 통화할 수 있을까요?)
2 You have the wrong number.
(전화 잘못 거셨어요.)
3 I can't answer the phone right now.
(지금은 전화를 받을 수 없습니다.)
4 May I leave a message? (메모 남겨도 될까요?)
5 Please tell her to call me back.
(그녀에게 저한테 전화해 달라고 전해주세요.)

Ⓒ Listen and fill in the blanks.

1 G: May I speak to Josh?
(Josh와 통화할 수 있을까요?)
   B: Speaking. Who's calling, please?
(전데요. 누구세요?)
   G: This is Sue. (나 Sue야.)

2 G: This is Julie. May I leave a message?
(저 Julie인데요. 메모 남겨도 될까요?)
   W: Sure. (물론이지.)
   G: Please tell Peter to meet me at 3, not 2.
(Peter에게 2시가 아니라 3시에 만나자고 전해주세요.)

3 G: This is Jessica. I can't answer the phone right now. Please leave a message.
(Jessica입니다. 지금은 전화를 받을 수 없습니다. 메모를 남겨주세요.)
   B: Hi, Jessica. This is Kevin. Please call me back after school.
(안녕, Jessica. 나 Kevin이야. 방과 후에 나한테 전화해줘.)

4 G: Hello? May I speak to Ben?
(여보세요? Ben과 통화할 수 있을까요?)
   B: My brother is not at home right now.
(동생은 지금 집에 없는데.)
   G: Okay. I'll call him back.
(알겠어요. 제가 다시 전화할게요.)
   B: Oh, don't hang up. He's home now. Hold on, please.
(오, 끊지 마. 그가 지금 집에 왔어. 잠시만 기다리렴.)

P.74~75 UNIT TEST

1 ⓐ hold on (전화를 끊지 않고 기다리다)
   ⓑ leave a message (메모를 남기다)
   ⓒ hang up (전화를 끊다)

ⓓ answer the phone (전화를 받다)

2 **B**: May I speak to Kate? (Kate와 통화할 수 있을까요?)
  W: She's not at home right now.
    (그녀는 지금 집에 없단다.)
  B: May I leave a message? (메모 남겨도 될까요?)
  W: Sure. Go ahead. (물론이지. 말하렴.)

3 ⓐ **G**: May I speak to Josh?
      (Josh와 통화할 수 있을까요?)
    B: Speaking. Who's calling? (전데요. 누구세요?)
  ⓑ **G**: May I leave a message? (메모 남겨도 될까요?)
    B: Sure. Go ahead. (네. 말씀하세요.)
  ⓒ **G**: May I speak to Josh?
      (Josh와 통화할 수 있을까요?)
    B: Sorry, but you have the wrong number.
      (죄송하지만, 전화 잘못 거셨어요.)
  ⓓ **G**: May I leave a message? (메모 남겨도 될까요?)
    B: Hold on, please. (잠시만 기다리세요.)

4 **G**: Hello? May I speak to Peter?
    (여보세요? Peter와 통화할 수 있을까요?)
  B: Who's calling, please? (누구세요?)
  G: _____
  ⓐ Speaking. (전데요.)
  ⓑ This is Susan. (저 Susan이에요.)
  ⓒ He's not here now. (그는 지금 여기 없어요.)
  ⓓ Hold on, please. (잠시만 기다리세요.)

5 **B**: Hello? This is Mike. May I speak to Jane?
    (여보세요? 저 Mike인데요. Jane과 통화할 수 있을까요?)
  G: She's not at home. (그녀는 집에 없어요.)
  B: May I leave a message? (메모 남겨도 될까요?)
  G: Sure. Go ahead. (물론이죠. 말씀하세요.)
  B: _____
  ⓐ I'll call her back. (제가 그녀에게 다시 전화할게요.)
  ⓑ Can we meet at 3 tomorrow?
    (내일 3시에 만날 수 있나요?)
  ⓒ Please tell her to meet me at the park.
    (그녀에게 공원에서 만나자고 전해주세요.)
  ⓓ I can't answer the phone now.
    (지금은 전화를 받을 수 없어요.)

6 ⓐ **W**: Who's calling, please? (누구세요?)
    M: This is Paul. (저 Paul이에요.)
  ⓑ **W**: May I speak to Kevin?
      (Kevin과 통화할 수 있을까요?)
    M: Hold on, please. (잠시만 기다리세요.)
  ⓒ **W**: May I leave a message? (메모 남겨도 될까요?)
    M: Sure. Please tell her to call me back.
      (물론이죠. 그녀에게 저한테 전화해 달라고 전해주세요.)

  ⓓ **W**: Isn't this 254-6253? (거기 254-6253 아닌가요?)
    M: No, it isn't. You have the wrong number.
      (아닌데요. 전화 잘못 거셨어요.)

7 (*Phone rings.*)
  M: Hello? (여보세요?)
  G: Hello? May I speak to John?
    (여보세요? John과 통화할 수 있을까요?)
  M: He's not here. Who's calling?
    (그는 여기 없단다. 누구니?)
  G: This is Kelly, John's friend. May I leave a
    message?
    (저 John의 친구 Kelly예요. 메모 남겨도 될까요?)
  M: Sure. (물론이지.)
  G: Please tell him to meet me at 6, not 4.
    (그에게 4시가 아니라 6시에 만나자고 전해주세요.)
  M: Okay. (그래.)

  Question: Which one is the correct message?
      (올바른 메모는 어느 것인가?)

8 (*Phone rings.*)
  W: Hello? (여보세요?)
  B: Hello? This is Ben. May I speak to Anna?
    (여보세요? 저 Ben인데요. Anna와 통화할 수 있을까요?)
  W: She's not at home right now.
    (그녀는 지금 집에 없단다.)
  B: May I leave a message? (메모 남겨도 될까요?)
  W: Sure. (물론이지.)
  B: Please tell her to call me back.
    (그녀에게 저한테 전화해 달라고 전해주세요.)
  W: Okay. Oh, wait. She's home now. Don't hang
    up, please. (*pause*) Anna, it's for you!
    (그래. 오, 기다리렴. 그녀가 지금 집에 왔단다. 끊지 말
    거라. Anna, 네 전화구나!)

  Question: What will the boy do next?
      (소년이 다음에 할 일은 무엇인가?)
  ⓐ He will leave a message. (그는 메모를 남길 것이다.)
  ⓑ He will hang up the phone.
    (그는 전화를 끊을 것이다.)
  ⓒ He will call Anna back.
    (그는 Anna에게 다시 전화할 것이다.)
  ⓓ He will talk to Anna on the phone.
    (그는 Anna와 통화할 것이다.)

UNIT 9 MY TOWN

ANSWERS

P.76

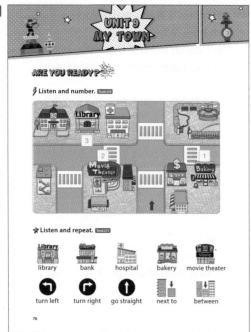

P.77

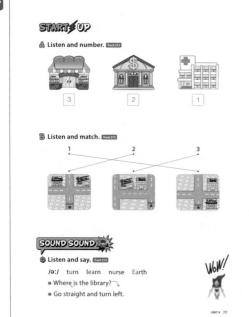

P.78

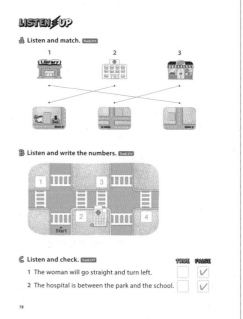

P.79

P.80~81 DICTATION

A   1 bakery   2 left   3 theater   4 right

B   1 straight   2 next, to   3 bank
    4 get, to   5 between

C   **1**   library, right
      2   there, get, turn, left
      3   hospital, Go, straight, between

    1 ⓑ   **2** ⓒ   **3** ⓐ   **4** ⓓ
    5 ⓒ   **6** ⓑ   **7** ⓑ   **8** ⓓ

SCRIPTS & 해석

P.76 ARE YOU READY?

⚡ **Listen and number.**

1 **B**: Excuse me. Where is the bakery?
(실례합니다. 빵집이 어디에 있나요?)
G: It's next to the bank. (은행 옆에 있어요.)

2 **B**: Excuse me. How can I get to the movie theater?
(실례합니다. 영화관에 어떻게 가면 되나요?)
G: Go straight and turn left. It will be on your left.
(똑바로 가서 왼쪽으로 도세요. 왼편에 있을 거예요.)

3 **B**: Excuse me. Where is the library?
(실례합니다. 도서관이 어디에 있나요?)
G: It's over there. It's between the school and the hospital.
(저쪽에 있어요. 학교와 병원 사이에 있어요.)

⭐ **Listen and repeat.**

library (도서관)   bank (은행)
hospital (병원)   bakery (빵집)
movie theater (영화관)

turn left (왼쪽으로 돌다)
turn right (오른쪽으로 돌다)
go straight (똑바로 가다)
next to (~ 옆에)
between (~의 사이에)

P.77 START UP

A **Listen and number.**

1 hospital (병원)
2 bank (은행)
3 bakery (빵집)

B **Listen and match.**

1 **G**: Where is the bank? (은행이 어디에 있나요?)

B: Go straight and turn right. It will be on your left.
(똑바로 가서 오른쪽으로 도세요. 왼편에 있을 거예요.)

2 **G**: How can I get to the library?
(도서관에 어떻게 가면 되나요?)
B: Go straight and turn left. It will be on your right.
(똑바로 가서 왼쪽으로 도세요. 오른편에 있을 거예요.)

3 **G**: Is there a movie theater around here?
(이 주변에 영화관이 있나요?)
B: Yes, it's next to the bank. (네, 은행 옆에 있어요.)

P.77 SOUND SOUND

🔵 **Listen and say.**

/əː/ turn (돌다)   learn (배우다)
     nurse (간호사)   Earth (지구)
🔵 Where is the library? (도서관이 어디에 있나요?)
🔵 Go straight and turn left.
(똑바로 가서 왼쪽으로 도세요.)

P.78~79 LISTEN UP

A **Listen and match.**

1 **M**: Excuse me. Where is the library?
(실례합니다. 도서관이 어디에 있나요?)
G: Go straight and turn right. It will be on your left.
(똑바로 가서 오른쪽으로 도세요. 왼편에 있을 거예요.)
M: Okay. Thank you for your help.
(알겠습니다. 도와주셔서 감사합니다.)

2 **B**: Excuse me. Where is the hospital?
(실례합니다. 병원이 어디에 있나요?)
W: It's over there. It's between the bank and the movie theater.
(저쪽에 있어요. 은행과 영화관 사이에 있어요.)
B: Thank you. (감사합니다.)
W: My pleasure. (천만에요.)

3 **G**: Excuse me. How can I get to the bakery from here?
(실례합니다. 여기서 빵집에 어떻게 가면 되나요?)
B: Go straight, turn left, and turn right. It will be on your left.
(똑바로 가서 왼쪽으로 돈 다음, 오른쪽으로 도세요. 왼편에 있을 거예요.)
G: Oh, I see. Thank you.
(오, 알겠습니다. 감사합니다.)

B Listen and write the numbers.

1 M: Excuse me. Where is the school?
(실례합니다. 학교가 어디에 있나요?)

G: Pardon? (뭐라고요?)

M: Where is the school? (학교가 어디에 있나요?)

G: Go straight and turn left. It will be on your right.
(똑바로 가서 왼쪽으로 도세요. 오른편에 있을 거예요.)

M: Oh, I see. Thank you.
(오, 알겠습니다. 감사합니다.)

2 W: Excuse me. Where is the bakery?
(실례합니다. 빵집이 어디에 있나요?)

M: Go straight and turn right.
(똑바로 가서 오른쪽으로 도세요.)

W: Pardon? (뭐라고요?)

M: Go straight and turn right. It's next to the hospital.
(똑바로 가서 오른쪽으로 도세요. 병원 옆에 있어요.)

W: Thank you very much. (정말 감사합니다.)

3 B: Excuse me. How can I get to the movie theater from here?
(실례합니다. 여기서 영화관에 어떻게 가면 되나요?)

G: Go straight, turn right, and turn left. Do you understand?
(똑바로 가서 오른쪽으로 돈 다음, 왼쪽으로 도세요. 이해하시겠어요?)

B: Go straight, turn right, and turn left.
(똑바로 가서 오른쪽으로 돈 다음, 왼쪽으로 도는 거죠.)

G: That's right. (맞아요.)

4 G: Excuse me. Is there a park around here?
(실례합니다. 이 주변에 공원이 있나요?)

B: Yes, there is. (네, 있어요.)

G: How can I get there?
(거기에 어떻게 가면 되나요?)

B: Go straight, turn right, and turn right again. It will be on your left.
(똑바로 가서 오른쪽으로 돈 다음, 다시 오른쪽으로 도세요. 왼편에 있을 거예요.)

C Listen and check.

1 W: Excuse me. Where is the bank?
(실례합니다. 은행이 어디에 있나요?)

M: Go straight and turn right.
(똑바로 가서 오른쪽으로 도세요.)

W: Pardon? Could you tell me again?
(뭐라고요? 다시 한 번 말씀해주실래요?)

M: No problem. Go straight and turn right. Do you understand?

(그럼요. 똑바로 가서 오른쪽으로 도세요. 이해하시겠어요?)

W: Yes. Thank you very much.
(네. 정말 감사합니다.)

M: My pleasure. (천만에요.)

Question: The woman will go straight and turn left.
(여자는 똑바로 가서 왼쪽으로 돌 것이다.)

2 M: Excuse me. How can I get to the hospital from here?
(실례합니다. 여기서 병원에 어떻게 가면 되나요?)

G: Pardon? (뭐라고요?)

M: How can I get to the hospital from here?
(여기서 병원에 어떻게 가면 되나요?)

G: Go straight, turn left, and turn left again. It's between the park and the library.
(똑바로 가서 왼쪽으로 돈 다음, 다시 왼쪽으로 도세요. 공원과 도서관 사이에 있어요.)

M: Oh, I see. Thank you.
(오, 알겠습니다. 감사합니다.)

G: You're welcome. (천만에요.)

Question: The hospital is between the park and the school.
(병원은 공원과 학교 사이에 있다.)

D Listen and write.

1 G: Excuse me. Is there a movie theater around here? (실례합니다. 이 주변에 영화관이 있나요?)

B: Yes, there is. (네, 있어요.)

G: How can I get there?
(거기에 어떻게 가면 되나요?)

B: Go straight and turn left. It will be on your left.
(똑바로 가서 왼쪽으로 도세요. 왼편에 있을 거예요.)

G: Okay. Thank you very much.
(알겠습니다. 정말 감사합니다.)

2 M: Excuse me. How can I get to the bakery?
(실례합니다. 빵집에 어떻게 가면 되나요?)

G: Go straight, turn left, and turn left again.
(똑바로 가서 왼쪽으로 돈 다음, 다시 왼쪽으로 도세요.)

M: Pardon? Could you tell me again?
(뭐라고요? 다시 한 번 말해줄래요?)

G: No problem. Go straight, turn left, and turn left again. It's between the bank and the school.
(그럼요. 똑바로 가서 왼쪽으로 돈 다음, 다시 왼쪽으로 도세요. 은행과 학교 사이에 있어요.)

M: Oh, I see. Thank you.
(오, 알겠습니다. 감사합니다.)

3 B: Excuse me. Where is the library?
(실례합니다. 도서관이 어디에 있나요?)

G: Go straight, turn left, and turn right.
(똑바로 가서 왼쪽으로 돈 다음, 오른쪽으로 도세요.)

B: Go straight, turn left, and turn right?
(똑바로 가서 왼쪽으로 돈 다음, 오른쪽으로 돌라고 요?)

G: That's right. It will be on your right.
(맞아요. 오른편에 있을 거예요.)

B: Thanks a lot. (정말 감사합니다.)

G: My pleasure. (천만에요.)

P.79 LET'S SPEAK WITH BUDDY

Listen and say.

Jenny: We're lost. (우리 길을 잃었어.)

Jack: Don't worry. (걱정하지 마.)

Jack: Excuse me. How can I get to the movie theater?
(실례합니다. 영화관에 어떻게 가면 되나요?)

Man: Go straight, turn right, and turn left.
(똑바로 가서 오른쪽으로 돈 다음, 왼쪽으로 돌거라.)

Jack: Pardon? (뭐라고요?)

Man: Go straight, turn right, and turn left. It's next to the bank.
(똑바로 가서 오른쪽으로 돈 다음, 왼쪽으로 돌거라. 은행 옆에 있단다.)

Man: Do you understand? (이해하겠니?)

Jenny: Yes! Thank you. (네! 감사합니다.)

P.80~81 DICTATION

A Listen and write the words.

1 bakery (빵집)
2 turn left (왼쪽으로 돌다)
3 movie theater (영화관)
4 turn right (오른쪽으로 돌다)

B Listen and write the words.

1 Go straight and turn left.
(똑바로 가서 왼쪽으로 도세요.)
2 It's next to the library. (도서관 옆에 있어요.)
3 Is there a bank around here?
(이 주변에 은행이 있나요?)
4 How can I get to the hospital?
(병원에 어떻게 가면 되나요?)

5 It's between the park and the school.
(공원과 학교 사이에 있어요.)

C Listen and fill in the blanks.

1 M: Excuse me. Where is the library?
(실례합니다. 도서관이 어디에 있나요?)

G: Go straight and turn right. It will be on your left.
(똑바로 가서 오른쪽으로 도세요. 왼편에 있을 거예요.)

M: Okay. Thank you for your help.
(알겠습니다. 도와주셔서 감사합니다.)

2 G: Excuse me. Is there a park around here?
(실례합니다. 이 주변에 공원이 있나요?)

B: Yes, there is. (네, 있어요.)

G: How can I get there?
(거기에 어떻게 가면 되나요?)

B: Go straight and turn left. It will be on your right. Do you understand?
(똑바로 가서 왼쪽으로 도세요. 오른편에 있을 거예 요. 이해하시겠어요?)

G: Yes. Thank you very much.
(네. 정말 감사합니다.)

3 M: Excuse me. How can I get to the hospital from here?
(실례합니다. 여기서 병원에 어떻게 가면 되나요?)

G: Pardon? (뭐라고요?)

M: How can I get to the hospital from here?
(여기서 병원에 어떻게 가면 되나요?)

G: Go straight and turn right. It's between the school and the bank.
(똑바로 가서 오른쪽으로 도세요. 학교와 은행 사이에 있어요.)

M: Oh, I see. Thank you.
(오, 알겠습니다. 감사합니다.)

G: You're welcome. (천만에요.)

P.82~83 UNIT TEST

1 ⓐ bank (은행)   ⓑ bakery (빵집)
ⓒ library (도서관)   ⓓ hospital (병원)

2 ⓐ The bank is next to the hospital.
(은행은 병원 옆에 있다.)
ⓑ The library is next to the bakery.
(도서관은 빵집 옆에 있다.)
ⓒ The bank is between the school and the library. (은행은 학교와 도서관 사이에 있다.)
ⓓ The library is between the school and the bank. (도서관은 학교와 은행 사이에 있다.)

3 **G**: Excuse me. How can I get to the movie theater from here?
(실례합니다. 여기서 영화관에 어떻게 가면 되나요?)

B: Go straight and turn left.
(똑바로 가서 왼쪽으로 도세요.)

G: Go straight and turn left?
(똑바로 가서 왼쪽으로 돌라고요?)

B: That's right. It will be on your right.
(맞아요. 오른편에 있을 거예요.)

4 **G**: Excuse me. Where is the bank?
(실례합니다. 은행이 어디에 있나요?)

M: Go straight and turn left.
(똑바로 가서 왼쪽으로 도세요.)

G: _____

ⓐ Do you understand? (이해하시겠어요?)

ⓑ You're welcome. (천만에요.)

ⓒ It's next to the library. (도서관 옆에 있어요.)

ⓓ Pardon? Could you tell me again?
(뭐라고요? 다시 한 번 말씀해주실래요?)

5 **W**: Excuse me. How can I get to the school?
(실례합니다. 학교에 어떻게 가면 되나요?)

B: Pardon? (뭐라고요?)

W: _____

ⓐ It will be on your left. (왼편에 있을 거예요.)

ⓑ Go straight and turn right.
(똑바로 가서 오른쪽으로 도세요.)

ⓒ How can I get to the school?
(학교에 어떻게 가면 되나요?)

ⓓ It's between the park and the bank.
(공원과 은행 사이에 있어요.)

6 ⓐ **B**: Where is the movie theater?
(영화관이 어디에 있나요?)

G: It's over there. (저쪽에 있어요.)

ⓑ **B**: Go straight and turn left. Do you understand?
(똑바로 가서 왼쪽으로 도세요. 이해하시겠어요?)

G: Sure. My pleasure.
(물론이죠. 도움이 되어 기뻐요.)

ⓒ **B**: Is there a park around here?
(이 주변에 공원이 있나요?)

G: Yes, there is. (네, 있어요.)

ⓓ **B**: How can I get there?
(거기에 어떻게 가면 되나요?)

G: Go straight and turn right.
(똑바로 가서 오른쪽으로 도세요.)

7 **M**: Excuse me. How can I get to the hospital from here?
(실례합니다. 여기서 병원에 어떻게 가면 되나요?)

G: Go straight, turn right, and turn left.
(똑바로 가서 오른쪽으로 돈 다음, 왼쪽으로 도세요.)

M: Pardon? (뭐라고요?)

G: Go straight, turn right, and turn left. It will be on your right. Do you understand?
(똑바로 가서 오른쪽으로 돈 다음, 왼쪽으로 도세요. 오른편에 있을 거예요. 이해하시겠어요?)

M: Yes, I do. Thank you very much.
(네, 이해했어요. 정말 감사합니다.)

G: You're welcome. (천만에요.)

Question: Where is the hospital?
(병원은 어디에 있는가?)

8 **B**: Excuse me. Where is the library?
(실례합니다. 도서관이 어디에 있나요?)

G: Pardon? (뭐라고요?)

B: Where is the library? (도서관이 어디에 있나요?)

G: Go straight and turn left, and turn left again.
(똑바로 가서 왼쪽으로 돈 다음, 다시 왼쪽으로 도세요.)

B: Go straight and turn left, and turn left again?
(똑바로 가서 왼쪽으로 돈 다음, 다시 왼쪽으로 돌라고요?)

G: That's right. It's next to the bakery.
(맞아요. 빵집 옆에 있어요.)

B: Thanks a lot. (정말 감사합니다.)

Question: The boy will go straight, <u>turn left, and turn left again</u>.
(소년은 똑바로 가서 <u>왼쪽으로 돈 다음, 다시 왼쪽으로 돌</u> 것이다.)

UNIT 10 PLANS

ANSWERS

P.84

P.85

P.86

P.87

P.88~89 DICTATION

A 1 travel   2 camping   3 haircut   4 study

B 1 going   2 shopping   3 plans
   4 relax   5 overseas

C 1 tomorrow, Chinese
2 weekend, camping
3 go, shopping, get, haircut
4 vacation, travel, visit, go, skiing

P.90~91 UNIT TEST

1 ⓐ 2 ⓒ 3 ⓐ 4 ⓓ
5 ⓑ 6 ⓒ 7 ⓑ 8 ⓓ

SCRIPTS & 해석

P.84 ARE YOU READY?

⚡ **Listen and number.**
1 **G**: What are you going to do tomorrow?
(내일 뭐 할 거니?)
B: I'm going to get a haircut. (머리를 자를 거야.)

2 **B**: Do you have any plans for your vacation?
(방학에 계획 있니?)
G: Yes, I'm going to go camping with my dad.
(응, 난 아빠랑 캠핑 갈 거야.)

⭐ **Listen and repeat.**
go shopping (쇼핑하러 가다)
get a haircut (머리를 자르다)
relax at home (집에서 쉬다)
go camping (캠핑 가다)
study Chinese (중국어를 공부하다)
travel overseas (해외여행을 하다)

P.85 START UP

Ⓐ **Listen and number.**
1 get a haircut (머리를 자르다)
2 study Chinese (중국어를 공부하다)
3 go camping (캠핑 가다)
4 travel overseas (해외여행을 하다)

Ⓑ **Listen and match.**
1 **B**: What are you going to do tomorrow?
(내일 뭐 할 거니?)
G: I'm going to go shopping. (쇼핑하러 갈 거야.)

2 **B**: Are you going to study Chinese this
weekend? (이번 주말에 중국어를 공부할 거니?)
G: No, I'm going to relax at home.
(아니, 난 집에서 쉴 거야.)

3 **B**: Do you have any plans for your vacation?

(방학에 계획 있니?)
G: Yes, I'm going to travel overseas.
(응, 난 해외여행을 할 거야.)

P.85 SOUND SOUND

🔊 **Listen and say.**
/i/ relax (쉬다)   review (복습하다)
become (되다)   before (~ 전에)
● What are you going to do tomorrow?
(내일 뭐 할 거니?)
● Do you have any plans for your vacation?
(방학에 계획 있니?)

P.86~87 LISTEN UP

Ⓐ **Listen and match.**
1 **G**: Peter, what are you going to do tomorrow?
(Peter, 내일 뭐 할 거니?)
B: I'm going to study Chinese. I have a test
next week.
(중국어를 공부할 거야. 다음 주에 시험이 있어.)

2 **B**: Amy, what are you going to do this
afternoon? (Amy, 오늘 오후에 뭐 할 거니?)
G: I'm going to get a haircut. (머리를 자를 거야.)

3 **B**: Lisa, what are you going to do this
weekend? (Lisa, 이번 주말에 뭐 할 거니?)
G: I'm going to go camping. I'm so excited.
(캠핑 갈 거야. 정말 신나.)
B: That sounds fun! (재미있겠다!)

Ⓑ **Listen and check.**
1 **G**: Do you have any plans for this Sunday?
(이번 주 일요일에 계획 있니?)
B: Yes, I'm going to go shopping. How about
you? (응, 난 쇼핑하러 갈 거야. 너는 어때?)
G: I'm going to get a haircut. I want a new
style.
(난 머리를 자를 거야. 새로운 스타일을 하고 싶어.)

2 **G**: What are you going to do for summer
vacation? (여름 방학에 뭐 할 거니?)
B: I'm going to take a trip with my family.
We're going to go to the mountains.
(가족과 여행을 할 거야. 우리는 산에 갈 거야.)
G: Are you going to go camping there?
(거기서 캠핑 갈 거니?)
B: Yes. I'm so excited. (응. 정말 신나.)

3 **G**: Do you have any plans for this afternoon?

(오늘 오후에 계획 있니?)

B: No, I don't. (아니, 없어.)

G: How about playing soccer together?
(같이 축구 하는 게 어때?)

B: Sorry, but I'm so tired. I want to relax at home.
(미안하지만, 난 너무 피곤해. 집에서 쉬고 싶어.)

G: Oh, okay. See you later then!
(오, 알겠어. 그럼 나중에 보자!)

4 B: Are you going to go to Kate's party this Friday?
(이번 주 금요일에 Kate의 파티에 갈 거니?)

G: No, I can't go. (아니, 난 못 가.)

B: Why not? Do you have plans?
(왜 안 돼? 계획 있니?)

G: Yes, I'm going to study Chinese. I have a test next Monday.
(응, 난 중국어를 공부할 거야. 다음 주 월요일에 시험이 있어.)

C Listen and check.

1 B: Do you have any plans for your vacation?
(방학에 계획 있니?)

G: Yes, I'm going to travel to Europe.
(응, 난 유럽 여행을 할 거야.)

B: Cool! What are you going to do there?
(멋지다! 거기서 뭐 할 거니?)

G: I'm going to visit museums. How about you? (박물관을 방문할 거야. 너는 어때?)

B: I'm going to go skiing with my family.
(난 가족과 스키 타러 갈 거야.)

G: Oh, that sounds exciting. Have fun!
(오, 재미있겠다. 즐거운 시간 보내!)

Question: The boy is going to go skiing for vacation.
(소년은 방학에 스키를 타러 갈 것이다.)

2 B: What are you going to do tomorrow?
(내일 뭐 할 거니?)

G: I'm going to relax at home. Do you have any plans? (집에서 쉴 거야. 넌 계획 있니?)

B: Yes, I'm going to get a haircut.
(응, 난 머리를 자를 거야.)

G: I want to get a haircut, too. Can I go with you?
(나도 머리 자르고 싶은데. 같이 가도 될까?)

B: Sure. See you tomorrow! (물론이지. 내일 보자!)

Question: The girl is going to get a haircut tomorrow.

(소녀는 내일 머리를 자를 것이다.)

D Listen and write.

1 G: Sam, are you going to visit your uncle for your vacation?
(Sam, 너 방학에 삼촌 댁을 방문할 거니?)

B: Yes, I am. (응, 그래.)

G: What are you going to do together?
(함께 뭐 할 거니?)

B: I'm going to go camping with my uncle's family. I'm so excited.
(삼촌네 가족과 캠핑 갈 거야. 정말 신나.)

2 G: Do you have any plans for your vacation?
(방학에 계획 있니?)

B: Yes, I'm going to study Chinese. How about you, Lily?
(응, 난 중국어를 공부할 거야. 너는 어때, Lily?)

G: I'm going to travel overseas with my family.
(난 가족과 해외여행을 할 거야.)

B: Cool! (멋지다!)

P.87 LET'S SPEAK WITH BUDDY

🔘 Listen and say.

Jack: Do you have any plans for your vacation?
(방학에 계획 있니?)

Tom: Yes, I'm going to go camping.
(응, 난 캠핑 갈 거야.)

Jack: That sounds fun! (재미있겠다!)

Tom: What are you going to do? (넌 뭐 할 거니?)

Jack: I'm going to go camping with you.
(난 너랑 캠핑 갈 거야.)

P.88~89 DICTATION

A Listen and write the words.

1 travel overseas (해외여행을 하다)

2 go camping (캠핑 가다)

3 get a haircut (머리를 자르다)

4 study Chinese (중국어를 공부하다)

B Listen and write the words.

1 What are you going to do this weekend?
(이번 주말에 뭐 할 거니?)

2 I'm going to go shopping.
(난 쇼핑하러 갈 거야.)

3 Do you have any plans for your vacation?
(방학에 계획 있니?)

4 Are you going to relax at home?
(너 집에서 쉴 거니?)

5 I'm going to travel overseas with my family.
(난 가족과 해외여행을 할 거야.)

C **Listen and fill in the blanks.**

1 G: Peter, what are you going to do tomorrow?
(Peter, 내일 뭐 할 거니?)

B: I'm going to study Chinese. I have a test next week.
(중국어를 공부할 거야. 다음 주에 시험이 있어.)

2 B: Lisa, what are you going to do this weekend? (Lisa, 이번 주말에 뭐 할 거니?)

G: I'm going to go camping. I'm so excited.
(캠핑 갈 거야. 정말 신나.)

B: That sounds fun! (재미있겠다!)

3 G: Do you have any plans for this Sunday?
(이번 주 일요일에 계획 있니?)

B: Yes, I'm going to go shopping. How about you? (응, 난 쇼핑하러 갈 거야. 너는 어때?)

G: I'm going to get a haircut. I want a new style.
(난 머리를 자를 거야. 새로운 스타일을 하고 싶어.)

4 B: Do you have any plans for your vacation?
(방학에 계획 있니?)

G: Yes, I'm going to travel to Europe.
(응, 난 유럽 여행을 할 거야.)

B: Cool! What are you going to do there?
(멋지다! 거기서 뭐 할 거니?)

G: I'm going to visit museums. How about you? (박물관을 방문할 거야. 너는 어때?)

B: I'm going to go skiing with my family.
(난 가족과 스키 타러 갈 거야.)

G: Oh, that sounds exciting. Have fun!
(오, 재미있겠다. 즐거운 시간 보내!)

P.90~91 **UNIT TEST**

1 ⓐ travel overseas (해외여행을 하다)
ⓑ go camping (캠핑 가다)
ⓒ relax at home (집에서 쉬다)
ⓓ get a haircut (머리를 자르다)

2 ⓐ She is going to go shopping.
(그녀는 쇼핑하러 갈 것이다.)
ⓑ He is going to relax at home.
(그는 집에서 쉴 것이다.)
ⓒ She is going to study Chinese.
(그녀는 중국어를 공부할 것이다.)

ⓓ He is going to go camping.
(그는 캠핑 갈 것이다.)

3 G: What are you going to do tomorrow?
(내일 뭐 할 거니?)

B: I'm going to get a haircut. I want a new style.
(머리를 자를 거야. 새로운 스타일을 하고 싶어.)

4 B: Do you have any plans for this weekend?
(이번 주말에 계획 있니?)

G: Yes, I'm going to visit my uncle. How about you? (응, 삼촌 댁을 방문할 거야. 너는 어때?)

B: _____

ⓐ I'm so excited. (정말 신나.)
ⓑ Do you have any plans? (너 계획 있니?)
ⓒ That sounds fun! (재미있겠다!)
ⓓ I'm going to relax at home. (난 집에서 쉴 거야.)

5 G: What are you going to do for your vacation?
(방학에 뭐 할 거니?)

B: I'm going to travel overseas. Do you have any plans? (해외여행을 할 거야. 넌 계획 있니?)

G: _____

ⓐ Sorry, but I can't. (미안하지만, 그럴 수 없어.)
ⓑ Yes, I'm going to study Chinese.
(응, 난 중국어를 공부할 거야.)
ⓒ Okay. See you later then.
(알겠어. 그럼 나중에 보자.)
ⓓ No, I'm not. (아니, 그렇지 않아.)

6 ⓐ B: What are you going to do this afternoon?
(오늘 오후에 뭐 할 거니?)
G: I'm going to get a haircut. (머리를 자를 거야.)
ⓑ B: Are you going to relax at home?
(너 집에서 쉴 거니?)
G: Yes, I am. (응, 쉴 거야.)
ⓒ B: Do you have any plans for winter vacation?
(겨울 방학에 계획 있니?)
G: That sounds exciting! (재미있겠다!)
ⓓ B: What are you going to do this Sunday?
(이번 주 일요일에 뭐 할 거니?)
G: I'm going to go skiing.
(스키 타러 갈 거야.)

7 B: I'm going to play soccer tomorrow. Do you want to play, too?
(난 내일 축구를 할 거야. 너도 하고 싶니?)

G: Sorry, but I can't. (미안하지만, 난 못해.)

B: Oh, do you have plans? (오, 너 계획 있니?)

G: Yes, I'm going to visit my grandmother. We're going to go shopping together.
(응, 할머니 댁을 방문할 거야. 우리는 함께 쇼핑하러 갈 거야.)

Question: What is the girl going to do tomorrow? (소녀가 내일 할 일은 무엇인가?)

8 B: What are you going to do this weekend?
(이번 주말에 뭐 할 거니?)

G: I'm going to relax at home. How about you?
(집에서 쉴 거야. 너는 어때?)

B: I'm going to go to the mountains with my family. (난 가족과 산에 갈 거야.)

G: Are you going to go camping there?
(거기서 캠핑 갈 거니?)

B: Yes. I'm so excited. (응. 정말 신나.)

Question: The boy is going to go <u>camping</u> this weekend.
(소년은 이번 주말에 캠핑 갈 것이다.)

P.92~93

REVIEW TEST 3 UNITS 7~10

| 1 ⓐ | 2 ⓓ | 3 ⓑ | 4 ⓑ | 5 ⓓ |
| 6 ⓐ | 7 ⓒ | 8 ⓑ | 9 ⓒ | 10 ⓓ |

1 ⓐ hold on (전화를 끊지 않고 기다리다)
ⓑ call back (다시 전화를 하다)
ⓒ hang up (전화를 끊다)
ⓓ leave a message (메모를 남기다)

2 ⓐ go camping (캠핑 가다)
ⓑ relax at home (집에서 쉬다)
ⓒ go shopping (쇼핑하러 가다)
ⓓ get a haircut (머리를 자르다)

3 B: How was your weekend? (주말 어땠니?)
G: It was fun. I visited my friend.
(재미있었어. 나는 친구를 방문했어.)
B: What did you do together? (같이 뭐 했는데?)
G: We played tennis. It was really fun.
(우리는 테니스를 쳤어. 정말 재미있었어.)

4 W: Excuse me. How can I get to the movie theater from here?
(실례합니다. 여기서 영화관에 어떻게 가면 되나요?)
M: Go straight and turn left.
(똑바로 가서 왼쪽으로 도세요.)
W: Go straight and turn left?
(똑바로 가서 왼쪽으로 돌라고요?)
M: _____
ⓐ Oh, I see. Thank you. (오, 알겠습니다. 감사합니다.)
ⓑ That's right. It will be on your right.
(맞아요. 오른편에 있을 거예요.)
ⓒ Sure. My pleasure. (물론이죠. 도움이 되어 기뻐요.)

ⓓ Pardon? Could you tell me again?
(뭐라고요? 다시 한 번 말씀해주실래요?)

5 B: I'm going to play soccer tomorrow. Do you want to play, too?
(난 내일 축구를 할 거야. 너도 하고 싶니?)
G: Sorry, but I can't. (미안하지만, 난 못해.)
B: Oh, do you have plans? (오, 너 계획 있니?)
G: _____
ⓐ Sorry, I'm so tired. (미안하지만, 난 너무 피곤해.)
ⓑ Yes. Can I go with you? (응. 내가 함께 가도 될까?)
ⓒ That sounds fun! (재미있겠다!)
ⓓ Yes, I'm going to get a haircut.
(응, 난 머리를 자를 거야.)

6 ⓐ B: May I leave a message? (메모 남겨도 될까요?)
G: He's not at home right now.
(그는 지금 집에 없어요.)
ⓑ B: What are you going to do this weekend?
(이번 주말에 뭐 할 거니?)
G: I'm going to go camping. (캠핑 갈 거야.)
ⓒ B: Where is the movie theater?
(영화관이 어디에 있나요?)
G: It's over there. It's between the bank and the bakery.
(저쪽에 있어요. 은행과 빵집 사이에 있어요.)
ⓓ B: What did you do last Tuesday?
(지난 화요일에 뭐 했니?)
G: I went swimming with my friend.
(친구와 수영하러 갔었어.)

7 ⓐ G: Are you going to relax at home this afternoon? (오늘 오후에 집에서 쉴 거니?)
B: No, I'm going to go shopping.
(아니, 쇼핑하러 갈 거야.)
ⓑ G: Go straight and turn right. Do you understand?
(똑바로 가서 오른쪽으로 도세요. 이해하시겠어요?)
B: Yes. Thank you very much.
(네. 정말 감사합니다.)
ⓒ G: Did you go to Tony's party yesterday?
(너 어제 Tony의 파티에 갔었니?)
B: No, I didn't. It was a lot of fun.
(아니, 안 갔어. 정말 재미있었어.)
ⓓ G: May I speak to John?
(John과 통화할 수 있을까요?)
B: I'm sorry. You have the wrong number.
(죄송하지만, 전화 잘못 거셨어요.)

8 M: Excuse me. How can I get to the hospital?
(실례합니다. 병원에 어떻게 가면 되나요?)
G: Go straight, turn right, and turn right again.

47

(똑바로 가서 오른쪽으로 돈 다음, 다시 오른쪽으로 도세
요.)

M: Pardon? Could you tell me again?
   (뭐라고요? 다시 한 번 말해줄래요?)

G: No problem. Go straight, turn right, and turn
   right again. It's next to the bakery.
   (그럼요. 똑바로 가서 오른쪽으로 돈 다음, 다시 오른쪽
   으로 도세요. 빵집 옆에 있어요.)

M: Oh, I see. Thank you. (오, 알겠습니다. 감사합니다.)

Question: Where is the hospital?
   (병원은 어디에 있는가?)

9 (*Phone rings.*)

M: Hello? (여보세요?)

G: Hello? May I speak to Nick?
   (여보세요? Nick과 통화할 수 있을까요?)

M: He's not at home right now. Who's calling?
   (그는 지금 집에 없단다. 누구니?)

G: This is Anna, Nick's friend. May I leave a
   message?
   (저 Nick의 친구 Anna인데요. 메모 남겨도 될까요?)

M: Sure. Go ahead. (물론이지. 말하렴.)

Question: What will the girl do next?
   (소녀는 다음에 무엇을 할 것인가?)

ⓐ She will call Nick back.
   (그녀는 Nick에게 다시 전화할 것이다.)

ⓑ She will answer the phone.
   (그녀는 전화를 받을 것이다.)

ⓒ She will leave a message.
   (그녀는 메모를 남길 것이다.)

ⓓ She will talk to Nick on the phone.
   (그녀는 Nick과 통화할 것이다.)

10 B: Do you have any plans for your vacation?
   (방학에 계획 있니?)

G: Yes, I'm going to study Chinese. How about
   you? (응, 난 중국어를 공부할 거야. 너는 어때?)

B: I'm going to travel overseas with my family.
   (난 가족과 해외여행을 할 거야.)

G: Oh, that sounds exciting. Have fun!
   (오, 재미있겠다. 즐거운 시간 보내!)

Question: The boy is going to <u>travel overseas</u> for
   vacation.
   (소년은 방학에 <u>해외여행을 할</u> 것이다.)

초등학생의 영어 친구
리스닝버디
LISTENING BUDDY 3

★리스닝버디의 특징

- **fun and friendly** 흥미로운 소재로 구성된 쉽고 재미있는 교재
- **step by step** 듣기 실력 향상을 위한 체계적인 구성
- **carefully prepared** 교육부에서 제시한 초등 교과과정의 의사소통 기능 반영
- **authentic language** 실생활에서 활용 가능한 대화 제시
- **productive** 발음 학습 및 speaking 활동을 보강하여 듣기와 말하기의 결합 강화

홈스쿨링 으로 빈틈없이 채우는 초등 공부 실력
세토 시리즈

신간 출시!

통합 학습역량 강화 프로그램

기초 학습서 초등 기초 학습능력과 배경지식 UP!   **교과 학습서** 초등 교과 사고력과 문제해결력 UP!

독서 논술	급수 한자	역사 탐험	초등 독해	초등 어휘	초등 한국사